Presented to Purchase College
by
Gary Waller, PhD Cambridge

State University of New York
Distinguished Professor

Professor
of Literature & Cultural
Studies, and Theatre &
Performance, 1995-2019
Provost 1995-2004

AN COLLINS

Divine Songs and Meditacions

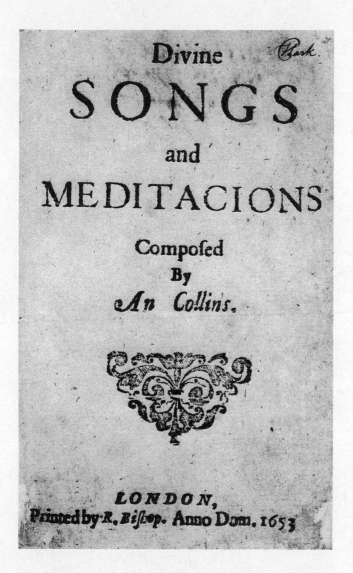

Medieval & Renaissance

Texts & Studies

Volume 161

RENAISSANCE ENGLISH TEXT SOCIETY

SEVENTH SERIES

VOLUME XIX (FOR 1994)

AN COLLINS

Divine Songs and Meditacions

Edited by

SIDNEY GOTTLIEB

MEDIEVAL & RENAISSANCE TEXTS & STUDIES
Tempe, Arizona
1996

Library of Congress Cataloging-in-Publication Data

Collins, An, 17th cent.
  Divine songs and meditacions / An Collins ; edited by Sidney Gottlieb.
    p.   cm. — (Medieval & Renaissance Texts & Studies; v. 161)
(Renaissance English Text Society; vol. 19)
  Includes bibliographical references.
  ISBN 0–86698–202–7 (clothbound)
  1. Christian woman—Religious life—Poetry. 2. Christian poetry, English.
Meditations. I. Gottlieb, Sidney. II. Title. III. Series. IV. Series: Renaissance
English Text Society (Series) ; vol. 19.
PR3349.C85D5 1996
821'.4—DC20   96–31028
                                                                                      CIP

This book was edited and produced
by MRTS at SUNY Binghamton.
This book is made to last.
It is set in Goudy typeface,
smyth-sewn, and printed on acid-free paper
to library specifications.

Printed in the United States of America

Contents

CONTENTS

Introduction

n Collins is in most respects a poet nearly anonymous. We know nothing about her apart from what we can glean from her one existing book, *Divine Songs and Meditacions* (1653), and although it contains an auto-biographical address to the reader and tantalizingly personal comments throughout the poems, this information is both skimpy and slippery. Her book is dated 1653 and published in London, but this still doesn't help us place her exactly: we don't know the circumstances of its publication, at what point in the author's life it was published (or indeed if it was published at or after her death, like the volumes of some other religious poets), when the poems in the volume were written, or where the author lived. Even her name (on the title page and at the end of "To the Reader") raises questions: Is "An" an unusual form of Ann or Anne, or an abbreviation of another name? Is it a personally styled or family name, or a printer's invention or corruption? At first glance, it may not even identify the author as a woman. "An" could, after all, refer to "Anthony" or some other such male name. Egerton Brydges, for example, in the earliest known critical comment on *Divine Songs and Meditacions* (in *Restituta*, published in 1815), begins by saying that "This very rare little volume is to be regarded as the production of a female," but acknowledges that he felt confident in reading "Anne" for "An" only after a passage referring to the author with feminine personal pronouns ten pages into the book seemed to authorize it (123). Brydges' hesitancy perhaps tells us something about the common habit of identifying authorship as "male," unless convinced otherwise, but it also reflects the real ambiguity and uncertainty that is attached to Collins' book from its opening page.

What, then, do we know — or imagine we know — about An Collins? From the evidence of her writings, she may have been sickly, even home-bound or bed-ridden. Physical affliction is a common trope for devotional writers, a predictable metaphor that helps describes the journey from this world to the next. But one senses that illness, weakness, and bodily pain were more than devotional or expressive devices for Collins, not only because of her specific references to having been "restrained from bodily employments," her "retired Course of Life" ("To the Reader"), and confinement to her house because of "weakness" ("The Preface"), but especially because the experience of pain and vulnerability is central in her poems, in all her attempts to understand her temporal and spiritual life. Suffering does not, of course, necessarily generate great or even interesting writing, and some of her verses are commonplace discourses on such topics as how "suffrings are of speciall use" ("A Song exciting to spirituall Alacrity," line 60). The following lines from her longest poem, "The Discourse," illustrate one of her common modes:

> Even in my Cradle did my Crosses breed,
> And so grew up with me, unto this day,
> Whereof variety of Cares proceed,
> Which of my selfe, I never could alay,
> Nor yet their multiplying brood destray,
> For one distemper could no sooner dy,
> But many others would his roome supply.... (57–63)

This is followed by an almost obligatory summoning up of "the messengers of *Iob*" (64), which still fails to add much interest to this particular tale of woe. But sometimes her complaints strike fire. The opening of "Another Song" ("Excessive worldly Greife"), for example, is not only a logical meditation on a familiar topic — that virtue is not rewarded and sometimes not even respected during one's lifetime — but it is also a haunting and emotionally exacting confession of how difficult it is to argue away the shame imposed by an unjust world:

Excessive worldly Greife the Soule devouers
And spoyles the activnesse of all the Powers,
Through indisposing them to exercise
What should demonstrate their abilities,
By practicall improvment of the same
Unto the Glory of the givers name.
Though Envy wait to blast the Blossoms green
Of any Vertu soon as they are seen,
Yet none may therfore just occasion take
To shun what Vertu manifest should make,
For like the Sun shall Vertu be beheld
When Clouds of Envy shall be quite dispeld;
Though there be some of no disart at all
Who no degree in worth can lower fall,
Prefer'd before the Verteous whom they taunt
Onely because of some apparent want,
Which is as if a Weed without defect
Before the Damask Rose should have respect,
Because the Rose a leafe or two hath lost,
And this the Weed of all his parts can boast;
Or elce as if a monstrous Clout should be
Prefer'd before the purest Lawn to see,
Because the Lawn hath spots and this the Clout
Is equally polluted thoroughout   (1–24)

We shall perhaps never know the details of what may well have been a physical disability underlying the experience described in these lines, but here and throughout the volume Collins finely anatomizes both physical and spiritual pain. Her faith always assures her that pain has both a meaning and an end, and this makes her, like George Herbert, a poet of not only the vagaries of but also recovery from affliction. But her knowledge of the ultimate triumph of the holy through God's abundant grace never effaces her sense of vulnerability. As we see in her finest poem of affliction, "Another Song" ("The Winter of my infancy"), which recalls Herbert both thematically and stylistically, the struggle to "persevere / In Piety and Holynesse" (56–57) is often a delicate balance of patient and anxious waiting, characterized by both unexpected disappointments and unexpected rewards.

But Collins is no mere statue of Patience, the traditional virtue of women trained or otherwise pressured to be, in the now well-known phrase, "chaste, silent, and obedient." In contrast to Helen Wilcox, who briefly describes Collins as a poet "who writes from an avowedly passive femininity" (56), and Elaine Hobby, who sees Collins as habitually "calling for retreat from argument" and retirement from public concerns (*Virtue of Necessity*, 60), I find much evidence of her boldness and engagement in public issues throughout the volume, and these qualities will be of particular interest to those studying Collins not only as an individual devotional poet but in the context of the development of women's "voices" in seventeenth-century England. Perhaps most obviously, her boldness is manifested in her repeated defense of her writing. While women in the seventeenth century were not often encouraged or prepared (that is to say, educated or given the material conditions) to write, and in fact were often actively discouraged from or criticized for writing, Hobby notes how frequently in Collins' volume "Writing is described . . . as a delightful and empowering activity for the author" (*Virtue of Necessity*, 59). Besides being an enjoyable task, one which she was "called" to, writing serves several worthwhile purposes: returning praise to God and testifying to God's grace and glory ("the fruits of righteousnesse / We to the glory of God must expresse," she says in "A Song shewing the Mercies of God to his people," 19–20); drawing "neare Kindred" ("The Discourse," 44) or others who may happen across the book closer to the Holy Scriptures, which figure prominently in the poems; and establishing her life as an exemplary model demonstrating that grace is given even to believers who are afflicted or of low status (see "The Discourse," 29–56).

Collins feels obligated to write and publish her writings, even though others of "sounder judgments" may be more capable and knowledgeable. She knows that she may be misunderstood, especially by those who read like a "spider," full of venom, but more sympathetic readers will surely excuse her defects and profit from her holiness and sincerity (see "The Preface," 79–98, 113–26). Further-more, she must write to show that she is not intimidated, discour-aged, or in any way stifled by the pressures of the ungodly or the recurrent frustrations in the rhythm of the holy life:

> Shall Sadness perswade me never to sing
> But leave unto Syrens that excellent thing,
> No that may not be....
> ("A Song demonstrating The vanities....." 1–3)

That simple but hard-earned "No that may not be" is a resounding anthem for a devotional poet, and especially so for one who is a woman.

Collins notes in several places how illness restricted her to home, but she resists this particular counterpart to the more perva-sive cultural relegation of women to the domestic sphere by com-menting throughout her poems on public issues and events. She may have been a beneficiary of the general freeing up of discourse during the Civil War period, which helped account for what Hobby calls "the first great outpouring of women's published writings in English" ("Discourse so unsavoury," 16), many of which address current affairs. In any event, personal and devotional issues often appear in historical and topical form or context in Collins' volume. For exam-ple, "A Song declaring that a Christian may finde tru Love only where tru Grace is" intimately and perhaps autobiographically describes "home debates, / And much domestick woes" (17–18) and failed friendships (74–96), and uses these as microcosmic illustrations to frame her analysis of the much broader social and public ruin caused by "the graceless crew" (65). Such poems as "A Song com-posed in time of the Civill Warr" (excluded by Stanley Stewart from his facsimile edition of selected poems by Collins "because its subject matter was not thought representative of the work as a whole" [iii]) and "Another Song" ("Time past we understood by story") directly focus on contemporary events, and other poems as well frequently allude to political and doctrinal innovations, social disruptions, and winters of discontent that are by no means purely personal matters. Throughout the poems she seems ready to take a strong stand on a variety of controversial theological as well as political topics that were debated at the time, such as the question of "mortalism" (whether or not the soul dies with the body), which figures in "A Song manifesting The Saints eternall Happinesse" and "Verses on the twelvth chapter of *Ecclesiastes*." Collins was evidently no believer in and certainly not silenced by the conventional notion that women were unsuited for commentary on public issues and political events.

In some ways the most pervasive sign of her boldness is her constant emphasis on knowledge, which both implicitly and explicitly contests the conventional pronouncements on women's limited intellectual capacity. In several places she issues a commonplace warning against "vain knowledge," part of her continuing argument against the misdirected energies of the ungodly, but one of the central premises of the entire volume is her statement in "The Discourse" that "holy Zeal ... must with knowledg dwell" (202). She is a deeply meditative poet, and her meditative method — which directs and structures not only the "Meditacions" near the end of her volume but several of the lyrics as well (e.g., "This Song sheweth that God is the strength of his People") — is based on finely developed skills of observation, rational analysis, and thoughtful judgment. These skills are perfectly consistent with faith, and help lead one to "right information" ("The Preface," 90) and "saving Knowledg" ("Another Song" ["Having restrained discontent"], 37). Throughout the volume, Collins' precepts and especially her example affirm that the acquisition of knowledge is every bit as much the woman's as the man's part.

While boldness, at least as I have described it, is indeed one of the most attractive characteristics of *Divine Songs and Meditacions*, I want to be careful not to overstate its significance. Margaret Ezell wisely emphasizes the dangers for editors, literary historians, and readers in general of worrying too much about whether "our literary forebears were 'good' feminists" (27). While the project of editing such poets as An Collins is to a great extent motivated and mandated by the current explosion of interest in more closely examining women writers, the most compelling reason for "recovering" her is not so much that she may be claimed as a prototypical feminist but that her writings, in Ezell's general formulation, help us to "glimpse the full complexity of the past" (165). I take this to mean that feminism, while rightly applauding all evidence of assertiveness, protest, and liberation, more generally recommends and facilitates a close examination of the self — particularly, although not exclusively, the female self — in history as both created and creative.

Accordingly, our interest in Collins should be an overdetermined one: multi-leveled, and broad as well as specific. We can engage with the volume and the author in any number of ways. The poems in *Divine Songs and Meditacions* are often stylistically and structurally interesting; some are prosaic and dully catechistical, but others are lyrical and dramatic. Collins is a sensitive meditative writer, a thoughtful commentator on key theological and political issues of her time, one who employs her poems not only to express but also to formulate her positions. She is an autobiographer of a self both tremulous and assured, suffering and singing, in the midst of spiritual and physical, public and personal pressures. These qualities make *Divine Songs and Meditacions* a wonderful rediscovery for the modern reader.

About the Text

The only known copy of the sole edition of *Divine Songs and Meditacions* (1653) is preserved at the Huntington Library, shelfmark RB 54047 (Wing C5355). In a brief note on Collins in his *Handbook to the Popular, Poetical, and Dramatic Literature of Great Britain*, W. Carew Hazlitt mentions a 1658 as well as the 1653 edition of this volume, but while other commentators occasionally repeat this reference, no one has ever confirmed the existence of a second edition of Collins' poems. (Hazlitt himself, in his earlier volume, *Second Series of Bibliographical Collections and Notes on Early English Literature 1474–1700*, recorded only the 1653 edition and said "No other is known.")

The volume is a small octavo, with a page size (cropped) of 136 x 83 mm at the largest dimension, bound in early nineteenth-century

English polished calf. It is made up of 52 leaves, gathered as follows: A, 4 leaves; B–G, each 8 leaves. The title page has been backed, presumably when the volume was rebound with blank filler leaves at the beginning and end. There is a signature in a mid-seventeenth-century hand at the top of the page headed "To the Reader," but while the first name "William" is clear, what follows is only partially decipherable, frustrating attempts to identify perhaps an early, or even the first, owner of the book. Other signatures and notations indicate later owners and track the progress of the book through different collections (described nicely by Stewart in the introduction to his facsimile, i): from Thomas Park, whose signature is in the book, to Thomas Hill, James Midgeley, Longman, and then to Mark Masterman Sykes, Thomas Thorpe, and Richard Heber. It was purchased at the Britwell Sale, March 31–April 4, 1924 by A. S. W. Rosenbach for Henry E. Huntington.

Perhaps the most interesting aspect of this genealogy of ownership is the trail of sale prices for this "unique" and apparently very costly volume. Hazlitt's summary (*Second Series*, 135) seems to tell a tale of declining value: "B. A. Poetica, 1815, £18, resold Midgley, 1818, £10, 10s., resold Sykes, 1824, £8, 5s., resold Heber, 1834, £4, 6s." But it was among the most expensive books listed in the *Bibliotheca Anglo-Poetica* catalogue of Longman collection books for sale, and in the catalog of the Sykes collection it was the most expensive book auctioned on one particular day, except for several early sixteenth-century multi-volume editions of Cicero bound in blue and red morocco. Even at £4. 6s. Heber was astonished. He registered his complaint in a note in the book: "I see nothing to justify so large a price for this vol[ume] – I much exceeded my com[missio]n. It is one of the dearest which I bought." The book was nearly "beyond" his range, "because it had been marked & sold at such absurd prices before."

The existence of only a single authoritative copy-text to work from simplifies some aspects of the process of editing Collins' poems. My aim is to present the text of the 1653 volume as exactly and accurately as possible, but I have made some adjustments in various features. I retain all original spelling, punctuation, italics, capital letters (including initial decorative or enlarged capitals), and indentation, but I have not reproduced word spacing variations or printer's ornaments. Long s is replaced by short s, vv is transcribed as w, turned letters are silently corrected, and abbreviations (specifically, three uses of "w^{ch}" and one tilde) are expanded. My textual notes call attention to a few likely errors in the original text and record necessary conjectures and corrections. When the original spelling or punctuation may be confusing to the modern reader, I offer explanations in my commentary. While modernizing the poems would make them more accessible in some ways, they are quite readable as they stand, and it is well worth preserving mid-seventeenth-century conventions, even though we may not be able to distinguish finally between those of the printer and those of the author. Spelling and punctuation are of course sometimes accidental, neutral, and, broadly speaking, insignificant, but other times they may serve important semantic, rhetorical, and expressive functions that modernizing would efface.

While editing a unique copy-text simplifies certain matters, it also introduces several problems. The print in the Huntington volume is very faint in some places and occasionally letters and punctuation marks are missing or barely visible. In addition, the volume is very tightly bound and cropped, so much so that on several pages letters are completely or partially cut off. In most cases, it is fairly easy to replace the missing letter with confidence, but in my textual notes I indicate a few instances where conjectures are a bit more problematic. Brydges reprints modernized selections from six of the poems in *Restituta*, and while he was working from the very same copy that I consulted, it may have been in better shape when he had it in his hands. His transcription of "Another Song exciting to Spirituall Mirth" is particularly valuable, since this is one of the poems with many missing letters. I have also checked my transcriptions against those in *Bibliotheca Anglo-Poetica*, Dyce, the modern anthologies *Kissing the Rod*, edited by Greer and Hastings, and *Her Own Life*, edited by Wilcox, and the typescript of the entire volume prepared by the Brown Women Writers Project, described as a Draft-in-Process. None of these is an authoritative text, but each one has

XV

corroborated various conjectures I have had to make and saved me from numerous errors in copying a sometimes very challenging seventeenth-century text.

About the Commentary

The poems of An Collins deserve and in some ways require a fully detailed critical commentary (which I am in the process of compiling for future publication), including extensive explanatory and interpretive notes, contextualizing information (and, inevitably, speculations) about the topical, doctrinal, gendered, and political dimensions of the poems, analysis of various technical and stylistic matters, and a variorum-type summary of the few critical works that mention Collins. For the purposes of the current volume, though, I have focused my commentary somewhat more narrowly. Here my emphasis is primarily on text-specific notes and glosses. Collins aims her book at the "Christian Reader" ("To the Reader"), one undoubtedly well-versed in the Bible, and she frequently includes biblical citations keyed to specific lines in her poems. I quote the relevant verses in full in the notes. Since the poems are deeply indebted to the Bible throughout, I note many places where her phrasing seems to echo a particular biblical passage, and I identify various biblical characters she mentions. (As with most seventeenth-century religious poets, though, it would be an almost endless task to note all biblical echoes, allusions, images, and references, so I have been somewhat selective.) I gloss various individual words, often to specify a seventeenth-century meaning of a word that might not be readily apparent to a twentieth-century reader, and paraphrase certain sections of poems where the meaning may be obscured by Collins' inverted sentence structures or what we might consider to be idiosyncratic punctuation. In addition, I cross-reference repeated uses of key words and topics, not only to sketch the development of certain themes but also to indicate how the poems help gloss one another.

Although we have no specific evidence about Collins' reading apart from the Bible and the unnamed "prophane Histories" alluded to in "To the Reader" and "The Discourse," (106–19), I occasionally gloss her poems with references to more familiar seventeenth-century religious writers, both before and after her time (e.g., Herbert, Vaughan, Milton). My intention is to relate her to various types of seventeenth-century literary discourse, not to assert specific debts, although we should not rule out the possibility of some direct influences. In several places I also try to compare Collins to other seventeenth-century women writers. Links of this kind are relatively new to me but are becoming increasingly vital and visible as more seventeenth-century women writers are edited and annotated.

In addition to text-based notes and glosses, while I try not to disguise a monograph as a series of notes, I do attempt to situate Collins in a variety of interpretive contexts, each of which poses certain problems. While I am well aware of the methodological dangers of and critical warnings against reading poetry autobiographically, Collins presents her writings as personal and experiential, and invites us to read the poems autobiographically. Whether we imagine a "self" behind the text or only the self constructed through the text, it is valid and valuable to be alert to the person, persona, and personality of An Collins, and in my notes I call attention to what seem to be the many signs of herself that she leaves in her poems.

She announces from the very beginning that her poems are devotional, and some of my comments highlight particular details of her religious beliefs and meditative style. That these beliefs are anything but transparently stated is illustrated by the fact that Collins has been variously identified as a Calvinist (Bell, Parfitt, and Shepherd, 53; Wilcox, 55), an anti-Calvinist (Norbrook, 881), and (perhaps) a Roman Catholic (Greer, 148). Throughout the commentary I briefly call attention to indications that she is, among other things, non-predestinarian, occasionally puritanical (a dangerously slippery term, but one that still retains some useful meaning), congregational as well as attuned to what she describes as a personal inner light, apocalyptic, and committed to continuing and reforming the Reformation. These qualities cut across many Protestant sects and churches, of course, but also make it worthwhile speculating on the extent to which Collins is, if not a Quaker herself, then at least deeply conversant in and attracted to much of what we associate with mid-seventeenth-century Quakers.

Although the poems are devotional — or perhaps *because* the poems are devotional, written during a time when religion and politics were inseparable — there are many topical and historical allusions throughout the volume which need to be identified and examined, a task I take up, again briefly and, of necessity, tentatively. Previous commentators on Collins' poems do not seem as divided about her political as they are about her religious beliefs, but I believe that Hobby, Stewart, and Wilcox overstate or oversimplify her conservatism. In the commentary I note instances of Collins' moral severity, calls for social and political order, and criticisms of various "radical" ideas, particularly those with possible antinomian implications. But I also call attention to the many indications of her deep commitment to the ongoing godly transformation of the world, which often puts her in sympathy with reformers and goals that are by no means "conservative." As with so many other writers, any truly useful assessment of Collins' political beliefs will have to embrace a complex matrix of ideas that do not reduce easily to the terms "radical" or "conservative."

Acknowledgments

I have received encouragement and advice on this project from Elaine Brennan, Norman T. Burns, Margaret J. M. Ezell, Elizabeth H. Hageman, Anne M. O'Donnell, and Helen Wilcox. The members of the New York Seventeenth-Century Seminar, directed by Diana Treviño Benet, offered very useful comments when I discussed with the group an early version of my editorial work and commentary. Ruth Kivette in particular alerted me to many biblical allusions that had eluded me.

I deeply appreciate the kind cooperation of the librarians at the Huntington Library while I examined the unique copy of Collins' poems, and I am grateful for their permission to reprint a facsimile of the title page. At the Huntington, Thomas V. Lange, Curator of

Early Printed Books and Bindings, and Mary L. Robertson, Curator of Manuscripts, helped me decipher the notes on the opening pages of the volume handwritten by various owners and book buyers, and at the very last minute Tom checked some final textual details and sent valuable information on the binding and physical characteristics of the book. Lisa Ann Libby, Rare Book Stacks Supervisor at the Huntington, also did some last-minute checking for me. A Folger Library short-term fellowship allowed me to move my work toward completion with a month of uninterrupted reading, transcribing, writing, and puzzling over the problems of editing such a text. While at the Folger, I benefitted greatly from almost daily conversations with Jean Klene, who was also working on an edition of a seven-teenth-century woman poet, Lady Anne Southwell.

Editing takes time and expertise, both of which I have had to scramble for. At Sacred Heart University, Judith Davis Miller, Thomas J. Trebon, and Kristen Wenzel helped with the former by arranging for released time and a convenient teaching schedule. And the supervising editorial committee of the Renaissance English Text Society, W. Speed Hill, John N. King, and Janel Mueller, added the latter to a project that was as "rough" as could be when it first came to them. Their corrections and suggestions improved this edition immeasurably, and Janel in particular, relentless and unerring, blue-pencilled my commentary not to death but to life, pointing out exactly how to go about doing what needed to be done. In the final stages of editing and production work once the volume was in the hands of MRTS, Mario A. Di Cesare helped ease me over the few remaining treacherous bumps. Working with this team confirmed for me that editing, like much scholarly work, can be demanding, tedious, and lonely, but also wonderfully cordial and collaborative.

AN COLLINS

Divine Songs and Meditacions

To the Reader

Christian Reader,

inform you, that by divine Providence, I have been restrained from bodily employments, suting with my disposicion, which enforced me to a retired Course of life; Wherin it pleased God to give me such inlargednesse of mind, and activity of spirit, so that this seeming desolate condicion, proved to me most delightfull: To be breif, I became affected to Poetry, insomuch that I proceeded to practise the same; and though the helps I had therein were small, yet the thing it self appeared unto me so amiable, as that it enflamed my faculties, to put forth themselvs, in a practise so pleasing.

Now the furtherances I had herein, was what I could gather (by the benifit of hearing,) at first from prophane Histories; which gave not that satisfactory contentment, before mencioned; but it was the manifestacion of Divine Truth, or rather the Truth it self, that reduced my mind to a peacefull temper, and spirituall calmnesse, taking up my thoughts for Theologicall employments.

Witnesse hereof, this Discourse, Songs and Meditacions, following; which I have set forth (as I trust) for the benifit, and comfort of others, Cheifly for those Christians who are of disconsolat Spirits, who may perceive herein, the Faithfullnesse, Love, & Tender Compassionatnesse of God to his people, in that according to his gracious Promise, *He doth not leave nor forsake them.* Heb. 13.5. *But causeth all things to work for theyr good.* Rom. 8.28. This I doubt not, but most Saints in som measure, do experimentally know, therefore I will not

1

seek by argument, to prove a thing so perspicuous. And now (Courteous Reader) I have delivered unto you, what I intended, onely it remaines that I tell you, That with my Labours, you have my Prayers to God through Jesus Christ; whose I am, and in him,

Yours,
in all Christian affection

AN COLLINS.

The Preface.

BEing through weakness to the house confin'd,
My mentall powers seeming long to sleep,
were summond up, by want of wakeing mind
Their wonted course of exercise to keep,
And not to waste themselves in slumber deep;
Though no work can bee so from error kept
But some against it boldly will except:

Yet sith it was my morning exercise
The fruit of intellectuals to vent,
In Songs or counterfets of Poesies,   [10]
And haveing therein found no small content,
To keep that course my thoughts are therfore bent,
And rather former workes to vindicate
Than any new concepcion to relate.

Our glorious God his creatures weaknesse sees,
And therefore deales with them accordingly,
Giveing the meanes of knowledg by degrees,
Vnfoulding more and more the Mystery,
And opening the Seales successively,   Rev. 6.
So of his goodnesse gives forth demonstracions,   [20]
To his Elect in divers Dispensacions.

In legall wise hee did himself expresse
To be the only Lord Omnipotent
A just avenger of all wickednesse,

3

A jelous God in power emminent,
Which terror workes, and pale astonishment;
Sith plagues for sin are holden forth thereby,
But with no strength to crush inniquity.

Now with the Law the Gospell oft appeares,
But under vailes, perspicuous unto few   [30]
Who were as those which of good tydings heares,
Rejoyceing much at the report or show
Of that the Saints now by possessing know;
Oft spake the Prophets Evangelicall,
Whose words like kindly drops of rain did fall.

But when the plenerie of time was come
The springs of grace their plesant streams out deald
Felicitie did evidence on her some
Salvacion and the way thereto reveald,
Who wounded were in spirit, might be heald;   [40]
Here God declares the Beauties of his Face,
Great Love, rich Mercy, free Eternall Grace.

This time was when the Sonne of Righteousnesse
His Luster in the world began to spread,
Which more and more to his he doth expresse
In tearms so large that they that run may read,
And to himselfe he doth the weaker lead;
He to his bosum will his Lambs collect,
And gently those that feeble are direct.   Isa. 40.11

And so in them a life of grace instill   [50]
Whereby they shall be able to obay
All Gospell precepts suting with his will,
And that without regard of servill pay,
But with free hearts, where Christ alone doth sway
Causing the apprehensions of his love,
To gender love, which still doth active prove.

4

Where Christ thus ruleth, I suppose remaines
No heart that hankers after Novelties
Whose ground is but the Scum of frothy braines
Perhaps extracted from old Heresies,   [60]
New form'd with Glosses to deceive the eyes
Of those who like to Children, do incline
To every new device that seemes to shine.

I am perswaded they that relish right,
The Dainties of Religion, Food divine,
Have therby such a permanent delight,
And of best Treasures, such a lasting mine,
As that their hearts to change do not incline,
I therfore think theyr tastes of Truth is ill,
Who Truths profession, quickly alter will.   [70]

I speak not this to manifest despight
To tru Religions growth or augmentacion,
Nor do I take offence of greater Light
Which brings probatum est, or commendacion
From Truth it selfe, having therto relacion,
But rather with the Saints I doe rejoyce,
When God appeares to his in Gospel-voyce.

Now touching that I hasten to expresse
Concerning these, the ofspring of my mind,
Who though they here appeare in homly dresse   [80]
And as they are my works, I do not find
But ranked with others, they may go behind,
Yet for theyr matter, I suppose they bee
Not worthlesse quite, whilst they with Truth agree.

Indeed I grant that sounder judgments may
(Directed by a greater Light) declare
The ground of Truth more in a Gospel-way,
But who time past with present will compare

5

Shall find more mysteries unfolded are,
So that they may who have right informacion   [90]
More plainly shew the path-way to Salvacion.

Yet this cannot prevayl to hinder me
From publishing those Truths I do intend,
As strong perfumes will not concealed be,
And who esteemes the favours of a Freind,
So little, as in silence let them end,
Nor will I therfore only keep in thought,
But tell what God still for my Soule hath wrought.

When Clouds of Melancholy over-cast
My heart, sustaining heavinesse therby,   [100]
But long that sad condicion would not last
For soon the Spring of Light would blessedly
Send forth a beam, for helps discovery,
Then dark discomforts would give place to joy,
Which not the World could give or quite destroy.

So sorrow serv'd but as springing raine
To ripen fruits, indowments of the minde,
Who thereby did abillitie attaine
To send forth flowers, of so rare a kinde,
Which wither not by force of Sun or Winde: [110]
Retaining vertue in their operacions,
Which are the matter of those Meditacions.

From whence if evill matter be extracted
Tis only by a spider generacion,
Whose natures are of vennom so compacted,
As that their touch occasions depravacion
Though lighting in the fragrantest plantacion:
Let such conceale the evill hence they pluck
And not disgorg themselves of what they suck.

6

So shall they not the humble sort offend   [120]
Who like the Bee, by natures secret act
Convert to sweetnesse, fit for some good end
That which they from small things of worth extract,
Wisely supplying every place that lackt,
By helping to discover what was meant
Where they perceive there is a good intent.

So trusting that the only Sov'rain Power
Which in this work alwaies assisted mee,
Will still remain its firme defensive Tower,
From spite of enemies the same to free   [130]
And make it useful in some sort to bee,
That Rock I trust on whom I doe depend,
Will his and all their works for him defend.

The Discourse.

YOu that indeared are to pietie,
And of a gracious disposicion are,
Delighting greatly in sinceritie
As your respects to godly ones declare;
For whose society you only care:
Dain to survay her works that worthlesse seem,
To such as honnest meanings dis-esteem.

But those that in my love I have preferd
Before all creaturs in this world beside,
My works, I hope, will never dis-regard,   [10]
Though some defects herein may be espide;
Which those that have their judgments rectifide:
Can but discern, yet not with scornfull eye,
As their mild censures cheefly testifie.

Vnto the publick view of every one
I did not purpose these my lines to send,
Which for my private use were made alone:
Or as I said, if any pious friend
Will once vouchsafe to read them to the end:
Let such conceive if error here they find,   [20]
Twas want of Art, not true intent of mind.

Some may desirous bee to understand
What moved mee, who unskilfull am herein,
To meddle with, and thus to take in hand,

That which I cannot well, end or begin;
But such may first resolve themselves herein,
If they consider, tis not want of skill,
Thats more blameworthy, than want of good will

1 Then know, I cheefly aim that this should bee
Vnto the praise of Gods most blessed name,   [30]
For by the mouths of sucking babes doth he,
Reveal his power, and immortall fame;   *Psal.* 8.
Permitting Children to extall the same:
When those that were profound, and worldly wise
In ignominious sort did him dispise.

2 Next in respect of that I have receiv'd
Is nothing to that some have, I do confesse,
Yet he to whom one Tallent was bequeath'd,
Was cald to strict account, nevertheless;
As well as he that many did possess,   *Mat.* 25.
From which I gather, they have no excuse,   [41]
Which of ability will make no use.

3 Moreover this is thirdly in respect
Of some neare Kindred, who survive mee may,
The which perhaps do better works neglect,
Yet this, they may be pleased to survay
Through willingnesse to heare what I could say,
Whereby they may bee haply drawn to look,
And read the Scriptures touched in this book.

4 And lastly in regard of any one,   [50]
Who may by accident hereafter find,
This, though to them the Auther bee unknown,
Yet seeing here, the image of her mind;
They may conjecture how she was inclin'd:
And further note, that God doth Grace bestow,
Vpon his servants, though hee keeps them low.

Even in my Cradle did my Crosses breed,
And so grew up with me, unto this day,
Whereof variety of Cares proceed,
Which of my selfe, I never could alay,   [60]
Nor yet their multiplying brood destray,
For one distemper could no sooner dy,
But many others would his roome supply,

Yea like the messengers of *Iob*, they hast,
One comes before another can be gon,
All mocions of delight were soon defast,
Finding no matter for to feed upon,
They quickly were disperced every one,
Whereat my minde it self, would much torment,
Vpon the rack of restless discontent.   [70]

The summers day, though chearfull in it selfe,
Was wearisom, and tedious, unto me,
As those that comfort lack, content or health,
To credit this may soon'st perswaded be,
For by experience truth hereof they see.
Now if the summers day, cause no delight,
How irksome think you was the winters night.

'Twere to no end, but altogether vain,
My several crosses namely to express,
To rub the scar would but encrease the pain,   [80]
And words of pitty would no griefe release,
But rather aggravate my heaviness,
Who ever chose my crosses to conseale
Till to my griefe they would themselves reveale

So (to be briefe) I spent my infantcy,
And part of freshest yeares, as hath been sayd
Partaking then of nothing cheerfully
Being through frailty apt to be affraid,

And likely still distempered or dismaid,
Through present sence of some calamity,   [90]
Or preconceipt of future misery.

But as the longest winter hath an end
So did this fruitlesse discontent expire,
And God in mercy some refreshing send,
whereby I learn'd his goodnesse to admire,
And also larger blessings to desire;
For those that once, have tasted grace indeed,
Will thirst for more, and crave it till they speed.

But that I may proceed Methodicall,
When first the restlesse wanderings of my minde,   [100]
Began to settle, and resolve with all
No more to be desturb'd with every winde
It such a pleasing exercise did finde,
Which was to ponder what Worth ech day,
The sence of Heareing should to it convay.

But liveing where profanenesse did abound,
Where little goodnesse might be seen or heard;
Those consolacions, could be but unsound
Haveing to godlinesse no great regard:
Because that of the means I was debard,   [110]
Through ignorance of better exercise
I then delighted plesant histories

Whereof the most part were but fain'd I knew
Which not-with-standing I no whit dispised,
Imagining although they were not true,
They were convenient being moralized;
Such vanities I then too highly prised:
But when profane discourses pleasd mee best
Obscenities I allwaies did detest.

11

But all this while, the fumes of vanities   [120]
Did interpose betwen my soules week sight,
And heavenly blisse, devine felicities;
Vntill that morning starr so matchlesse bright
The Sun of righteousnesse reveald his light
Vnto my soule, which sweet refreshings brings,
Because he coms with healing in his wings.   *Mal* 4 2

Whose blessed beames my mind eradiates
And makes it sensible of pietie,
And so by consequence communicates
Celestiall health to ev'ry faculty: [130]
Expeling palpable obscurity;
Which made my soule uncapable of grace,
Which now she much desires for to imbrace.

Perceiving well that nothing can afford
Her either finall rest, or full content,
But saveing Graces, and Gods holy word,
Which is a means those Graces to augment;
With Praier, and the blessed Sacrament:
Which means with reverence my soul affects
And former pleasing vanities rejects.   [140]

Together with unnecesary griefe,
Whose ill effects can hardly bee exprest,
For certainly it argues unbeleife
Which hinders many from eternall rest,
who do not seek in time to be redrest;   *Heb.* 3.19
Therefore I would establish inward peace,
How-ever out-ward crosses do increase.

If cross disgrace or dismall accident,
Indignity or loss, befalleth mee,
Immediatly distempers to prevent,   [150]
I cald to mind how all things orderd bee,

12

Appointed, and disposed, as we see,
By Gods most gracious providence, which is,
I am perswaded, for the good of his.

Yet am I not so firm I must confess
But many times discomforts will intru'd,
Which oft prevailes to hinder quietness,
And by that means, some sorrows are reneu'd:
Which hope will help mee quickly to exclu'd:
So though distress continu for a night,   *Psal.* 30. 5
Yet joy returneth by the morning light.   [161]

With confidence these favours will increase
My soule hath recolected all her powers,
To praise the auther of this blissfull peace,
Which no untimely crosse event devouers;
So permanent are the celestiall Flowers:
Those graces which are ever conversent,
Where holyness combinds with true content.

O! what trancendant ravishing delights
What blis unspeakable they doe posesse,   [170]
Whose merth to holy praises them excites,
And cheers them to go on, in godlynesse,
The very quintisence of happinesse,
As is attainable, or may be had
In this life present, which were elce but bad.

There is a kind of counterfet content,
Wherwith some are deceivd, tis to be feard,
Who think they need not sorrow, or lament,
Being to sensuall pleasures so indeard;
Whose minds are stupid, & their concience ceard   [180]
Elce might they see all Earthly delectatcion,
To be but vanity, and hearts vexacion.   *Eccl.* 2.

13

To lightning, carnall merth we may compare,
For as a flash it hastes and soon is gon,
Foretelling of a Thunder clap of care,
It also blastes the heart it lighteth on;
Makes it to goodnesse, senceless as a ston:
Disabling every part, and faculty,
Of soul and body unto piety.

But sacred joy is like the Sunnes clear light,   [190]
Which may with clouds, be sometimes overcast,
Yet breaks it forth anon, and shines more bright,
Whose lively force continually doth last;
And shews most Orient, when a storm is past:
So true delight may bee eclips'd we see,
But quite extinguisht, can it never bee.

So now I will go on with my Discourse,
When knowledg, plesant to my soul became,
Unto Gods word, I often had recourse,
Being informed rightly that the same;   [200]
Would bee as fuell to encreace the flame
Of holy Zeal, which must with knowledg dwell,
For without other, neither can do well,   *Rom.* 10

Then sought I carefully to understand,
The grounds of true Religion, which impart
Divine Discreshion, which goes far beyand,
All civill policy or humane Art;
Which sacred principles I got by heart:
Which much enabled me to apprehend,
The sence of that whereto I shall attend.   [210]

First touching God, there is one God I know,
who hath his being of himself alone,   *Rom.* 1. 20.
The fountain whence al streams of goodnesse flow
But body, parts, or passions hath he none;   *Ia.* 1 7

14

And such a Diety, there is but one;   1 *Cor.* 8. 4.
Eternal, Infinite, alone is hee,   1 *Iohn.* 5.7.
One perfect Essence, distinct Persons Three.

The first whereof, for order, is the Father,
The Glorious Fountain of the Trinity,
Having his being, nor begining neither   [220]
Of no one but himselfe, undoubtedly;
Begets his Sonne, from all eternity,
And with his Sonne, the Holy-Ghost forth sends
From ever-lasting which for aye extends.

The Sonne, the second Glorious person is,
For Power, Substance, and Eternity,
Alone as is the Father, who it is,
Of whom he hath his being, too, only;
Yea the whole being of his Father, by
A Sacred and Eternall Genneracion,   [230]
A mistrey past all imaginacion.   *Isaiah.* 53. 8

In Trinity the Holy-Ghost is third,
Proceeding and so sent forth equally,   *Iohn.* 15.7.
Both from the father & the son, or word,   *Iohn.* 1.1
Being of their Power, Substance, Magisty;
And thus distinguished are the Trinity:
By whom were all-things made, that ever were,
And by whose Providence preserved are.

What hath been sayd of God shall now suffice,
Of whom I frame no Image in my mind,   [240]
But I conceive him by his properties,
Hee is incomprehensible I find;
Filling all places, in no place confind;
I will therefore his wondrous works admire,
Not vainly after secret things inquire.

15

Next unto God, my selfe I sought to know,
A thing not so facile, as some suppose,
But that I may the faster forward goe,
I leave to speak, what may bee said of those,
And haste to that I purpose to disclose: [250]
Which being well considered may convert,
To lowest thoughts, the proudest haughty heart.

Touching my selfe and others I conceive,
That all men are by nature dead in sin,   *Eph.* 2.1.
And Sathans slaves; not able to receive,
The things of God, which brings true comfort in:
Good accions still they faile in managing,
But apt they are to every vanity,
As vowed servants to inniquity.

Doe but observe the carnallist how he   [260]
Neglects all calings, fitt to be profest,
Waits all occasions, ill imployd to be,
Consumes his wealth, deprives himself of rest;
To please that darling sinn that likes him best:
Iudg what a hellish bondage he is in,
That's Sathans slave, and servant unto sin;

As all men in the state of nature be,
And have been ever since mans wofull fall,
Who was created first, from bondage free,
Untill by sinn he thrust himself in thrall;   [270]
By whose transgression we were stained all,
Not only all men but all parts of man,
Corrupted was: since sin to reign began.

The Soul who did her makers Image bear,
Which made her amiable fair and bright,
Right Orient and illustrious to appear,
To his omniscient eye and pure sight,

Who doth the inward Purity delight,
Lost all her beauty, once so excellent,
As soon as unto sinn she did consent.   [280]

The eye of understanding was so bleared,
That no spirituall thing it could behold,
The will corrupted, and the concience ceared,
And all th'affections were to goodness cold,
But hot to evill, not to be contrould;
The members of the body then proceeds
As instruments to execute bad deeds.

But see what was the consequence of this,
The curse of God which did the fault ensue,
Thus man by sin deprived was of bliss,   [290]
The thoughts hereof might cause us to eschew
That bitter root whence all our sorrows grew:
Sickness of body, and distresse of mind,
With all afflictions layd upon mankind.

Whether in body goods or name it be,
And which is worce, the soules perplexity,
Whose concience is awake, from deadnesse free
When she considers what felicity,
She hath exchang'd for endlesse misery;
Can but torment her selfe with bootlesse care,   [300]
Fore-see-ing that her pains eternall are.

If this be so, the vilest liveing creature
Is in better case then man; for why?
When this life ends with such by course of nature,
There with is ended all his misery;
But man tormented is eternally;
Twere so, but that our God we gracious find,
Who sent a Saviour to restore mankind.

The second person of the Trinity,   *Iohn.* 1.1
The only Son of God omnipotent,   [310]
Who being God from all eternity,
To take our nature freely did assent,   *Heb.* 2.16.
With all afflictons thereto insident:
In all things like to other men was he,
Save that from sins he still remained free.

So that two whole and perfect natures were,
In the same person joyned really.
And neither of them both, confounded are,
Nor doth the Humane of it selfe rely;
But it subsisteth in the Deity,   [320]
Nor can these natures seperated be,
Both perfect God, and perfect man was he.

This much touching our Saviours person; Now,
His Offices we ought to know likewise,
And what he hath performd for us, and how
He freed us from the foresaid miseries,
And how Gods dreadfull wrath he satisfies;
His Offices shall briefly named be,
A Priest, a Prophet, and a King, is he.

A Priest, for that he hath for mans transgression   [330]
Full satisfaction made to God the father,   *Heb.* 7.15.
And likewise makes continuall intercession,
For those who to his fould he means to gather;
Or to eternall heavenly mancions, rather:
The means wherby Gods wrath he satisfies,
Was his obedience and his sacrifice.

The Law of God he perfectly fulfild,
With full obedience and integrity,
As God had pre-ordained, then did he yeild
A painfull ignominious death to dy,   [340]

The wrath of God appeased was thereby,
Which in full measure came upon him then,
Even what was due unto the sins of men.

A Prophet to instruct his Church he is,
Which doth him honour by sinceare profession,
His Spirit qualifies the hearts of his,
And makes them pliable to such profession,
His word doth take when grace shall have possession,
For by the word no good efect is wrought
But where the heart is by Gods spirit taught.   [350]

Our Saviour is a King undoubtedly,
Although he seemes to have no Kingdoms here,
Yet in their hearts he means to Glorify,
A Kingdome he erects of grace, and there
Hee raignes, and by his spirit rule doth beare,
But here appears his machlesse dignity
Hee King of Glory is Eternally.

For when he by his death had finished
The work of our redemcion, freed from paines,
He took his body that before was dead,   [360]
With all that to a perfect man pertaines;
With which he gloriously ascends and reignes:
At the right hand of God he doth remain
Vntill to Iudgment he returns again.

Christs sufferings are sufficient for to free,
All men from wo and endlesse misery,   2 Thes. 3.2
But all men have not faith, and therfore be,
Vnlikely to have benefit thereby,
For it is Faith with which we must apply,
The merrits of our blessed Redeemer   [370]
And to our selves each in particuler.

Faith is a Grace which doth the soul refine,
Wrought by the Holy-Ghost in contrite hearts,
And grounded on Gods Promises divine,
Things superexcellent this same imparts,
To those that have it planted in their hearts:
But ere this faith is wrought, the heart must be,
Made capable of it, in some degree.

First God doth take the hammer of his Law,
And breaks the heart which he for Grace will fitt   [380]
Then the seduced soul is brought in aw,
And doth immediatly it selfe submitt,
When sight of sinne, and sorrowing for it,
Hath wrought humility, a vertu rare
Which truly doth the soul for Grace prepare.

The Law of God is most exact and pure
Requireing of us perfect holinesse,   *Psal.* 19.1
To which is life eternall promis'd sure,
But curses unto them that it transgresse,
Whether by frailty or by wilfullnesse;   [390]
Though none but Christ, and *Adam* ere his fall
Could keep this Law, yet it may profit all.

For here we may perceive how much we fail,
Withall what danger we incur thereby,
Then if we can our own defects bewail,
We may for succur to our Saviour fly,
Whose Righteousnesse will all our wants supply:
Then here are Rules set down for Gods Elect
Whereby they will their course of life direct.

This Law by Gods most skilfull Hand was wrot,   [400]
And placed in two Tables orderly,
Shewing what's to be done, and what is not;
Withall what good or evill coms thereby,

20

In Ten Commandements so distinctly,
Wherewith as with a Touch stone try we may,
How we offend our God, or him obay.

1 They sin against the first who think or say,
As doth the fool, there is no God at all,
So they that through profanenesse disobay,
And want of knowledge is a breach not small,   [410]
Who loves or fears a creature most of all,
And puts trust therein and seeks there-to
Makes that their God, and so break this they do.

2 The second violated is by those
That Images erect, or them adore,
By such also who in devocion goes
To Saint or Angell, succor to implore,
Who set by superstitious Reliques store,
And worship God after mens fantasies,
And not as he commands, breaks this likewise   [420]

3 When those that seem religious prove profane,
Gods name is much dishonoured therby;
Even so likewise their error is the same,
Who use his word, or works, or Titles high,
For evil ends, or elce unreverently:
By witchcraft, cursing, swearing, blasphemy,
This violated is undoubtedly.

4 Whoso by preparation doth not fit
Himselfe to keep the Sabbath, breaks the same,
As those that holy exercise omit,   [430]
Or come thereto only for fear of blame,
Nor have delight or profit by the same;
So it is broke by carnall recreations,
By worldly works, by speech, or cogitacions.

21

5 When that inferiors disobedient are,
Vngratefull, stubborn, saucy, impudent,
Fayling in reverence, love, respective care,
To their superiors, hating Government,
Such grosly break this Fift Commandement:
As those superiors whose bad Disciplin   [440]
Or ill example, makes inferiors sin.

6 This is transgrest by murther, or debate,
By being mindfull of revenge likewise,
By sinfull anger, envy, malice, hate;
By vexing words, and scornfull mockeries,
Which are occasions of extreamities,
Distresse of mind, heart-griefe, perplexity,
And life hath often prejudice thereby,

7 All thoughts impure this Command'ment breaks,
So lewd pastimes, light gesture, wanton lookes,   [450]
Wearing apparell contrary to Sex,
Ill company, vain talk, lacivious books,
And all that may entice like baites or hooks,
To Fornication or Adultery,
Which breakes this Precept most apparently.

8 This is transgrest by any kind of stealing,
By coveting our nighbours goods also,
By fraud, oppression, or deceitfull dealing,
By not disposing well of that we ow,
Refusing honest works to undergoe,   [460]
By being not content with our estate,
Not helping those we should commiserate.

9 This violated is by false witnesse bearing,
Likewise by any Lie we break the same,
By raiseing false reports, or gladly hearing
Ill of our nighbour, touching his good name,

By not maintaining his deserved fame,
By speaking truth of him maliciously
And not exhorting him in secresie.

10 This is transgrest by lusts, and mocions vain   [470]
Though we thereto give no consent at all,   *Ro.* 7.7
As the rebellion of the flesh, or stain
And blot, we have by sinne Originall,
Corruption of our nature we it call;
From which because that no one can be free,
Then all transgressors of the Law must be.

Who by the morrall Law beholds his sin
And sees withall ther's left him no defence,
To sorrow therefore now he doth begin,
His Conscience being toucht with lively sence   [480]
Of Gods displeasure for his great offence,
Dispairing of salvation, in respect
Of ought that by himselfe he can effect.

The curse contain'd in this exquiset Law,
Doth work this sorrow so effectually,
For truly he alone is brought in aw,
Whose Conscience is inform'd of this hereby;
Who breaks but one commandement only
In all his life, and that in coggitacion,
Is not-with-standing subject to damnacion.   [490]

Thus when the heart is fitted and prepard,
The seeds of Faith forth-with are cast therein,
Which in their orders briefly are declard:
The first is when one wearied under sinne,
To feel the wiaght thereof doth now begin
And thereupon acknowledgeth with speed
That of a Saviour much he stands in need:

The second is a vehement desire,
Or ardent longing to participate
Of Christ, and eke his benifits entire   [500]
And nothing else can this desire abate,
Consume or limit, quench or mittigate:
As doth the Hart the water brook desire,
So humble Souls a Saviour doth require.

The third is flying to the Throne of grace,
Even from the sentence of the Law so strict,
Which doth profane security deface,
Because that thereby the Conscience is prict,
Which doth the humble man for good afflict
By shewing such the danger of their case,   [510]
And for a cuer, sending them to grace.

Now this is done by fervent supplications,
By constant prayer, most prevailing known,
Exprest with hearty, strong ejacculacions,
For Gods especiall grace in him alone,
In the forgivenesse of his sins each one;
And in his prayer, persevear will hee
Vntill the thing peticion'd, granted bee.

Then God, as he hath promised, will prove
Propicious to the sinner penitent,   [520]
And let him feel th'assurance of his Love,
His Favour, Grace, and Mercy Excellent
The which in Christ, appears most emminent:
A lively Faith this full assurance is,
Wrought by Gods Spirit, in the hearts of his.

But there are divers measures or degrees
Of Saving Faith, the least whereof is this,
When he that hath a humble Spirit sees
He cannot feel, his Faith so little is,

24

As yet the full assurance, inward bliss,   [530]
Of the forgivenesse of his sinnes so free,
Yet pardonable findeth them to bee.

And therefore prayeth they may be pardoned,
And with his heart the same of God requires,
Recals himself, as formerly misled,
Giveing no rest unto his large desires,
His Soul it faints not, nor his Spirit tires,
Although he be delayd yet still he praies,
On God he waites, and for an answer staies.

That such a man hath Faith it doth appeare   [540]
For these desires doe plainly testifie,
He hath the Spirit of his Saviour dear,
For tis his speciall work or property,
To stir up longings after purity:
Now where his Spirit is there Christ resides,
And where Christ dwels true Faith though weak abides

Of saveing Faith the largest quantity,
Is when a man comes on in Faith untill,
He finds the full assurance happily
Of Gods free mercy, favour, and good will,   [550]
To him in Christ, which doth his joy fulfill:
Finding he hath obtained free remission,
And that he's safe in Gods divine tuision.

This full assurance of his grace and love,
The Lord vouchsafes his servants true who he,
Doth for their inward sanctity approve,
Whose outward doeings also righteous be,
For such alone the evidence may see,
Of his inheritance, true happinesse,
Which for Christs merits sake they shall possesse.   [560]

A Christian in his infantcy in grace
Finds not this full assurance usually,
Vntill he hath been practis'd for a space
By sound Repentance with Sincerity:
And finds Gods Love to him abundantly
Then shall his soul this full perswasion see,
Which is the strength of Faith or highest degree.

By Faith in Christ much profit we do gain,
For thereby only are we justifide,
At peace with God free from eternall pain,   [570]
And thereby only are we sanctifide,
Where faith is, by those fruits, it may be tride:
True faith being by fruits discovered
A barren faith must needs be false and dead.

Now to be justifide, is to be freed,
From gilt and punishment of sin likewise,
To be accepted as for just indeed,
With God, whose grace it is that justifies;
And not our works, as vainly some surmise:
But that we may still orderly proceed,   [580]
It followeth next how we from sin are freed.

The sins of those that God will justifie,
Were by Christs sufferings so abolished,
As that they cannot hurt them finally,
Were they as Scarlet or the Crimson Red,   *Esay.* 16. 16
They shall be white as Snow and cleared,
Even by Christs Blood, the which to free was spent
The faithfull, from deserved punishment.

Now comes to be considered how they may
With God, for Perfect-just, accepted be,   [590]
Who of them-selves by nature (truth to say)
Are in no part from sinnes corruption free,

26

How such are tane for just, here may we see,
Christs righteousnesse is theirs, by imputacion,
And so esteem'd by gracious acceptacion.

The true beleevers benifits are great,
Which they by being justifide possesse
For such shall stand before Gods judgment seat,
As worthy of Eternall Happinesse,
Even by the merits of Christs Righteousnesse,   [600]
For of themselves, they cannot merit ought,
Who are not able to think one good thought.

Then far from doing any work whereby
They might deserve Salvation on their part,
For God whose only perfect purity,
Will find in our best works no true disart,
But rather matter of our endlesse smart:
For in Christs Blood the Saints which are most dear
Must wash their Robes before they can be clear.

Though by good works we do not gain Salvacion   [610]
Yet these good Duties that our God requires,
We must perform in this our conversacion,
With all our might, endevours, and desires,
Before this short uncertain time expires,
And at perfection must we allwaies aime,
Though in this life we reach not to the same.

For he that by his Faith is justifide,
It followeth also necessarily,
That such by Faith are likwise Sanctifide,
Corrupcion of our nature is thereby   [620]
Disabled so, as that inniquity
No longer rules, being by grace subdude,
Whereby the heart to goodnesse is renude.

27

Corrupcion of our nature purged is,
By vertue of Christs Precious Blood only
Which when by Saving Faith applyed is,
Serves as a corrasive to mortifie
And kill the power of inniquity,
Whence tis that those who Sanctified bee,
From sins dominion, happily are free.   [630]

The other part of true Sanctificacion,
Is life or quickenning to holinesse,
And may therefore be called renovacion,
Like a Restorative it doth redresse,
And him revive, that is dead in trespasse;
Tis by the power of Christs Resurrection,
That we are rais'd from sinne to such perfection.

Sanctificacion must be then entire,
Not for the present, perfect in degree,
Yet in respect of parts and true desire,   [640]
Each part and power Sanctified must bee,
Although no part from all Corruption's free;
Yet every power must with goodnesse sute,
Though in this life no part be absolute,

Like as a Child new born without defect,
A perfect man he may be sayd to bee,
Because his body's perfect, in respect
Of parts, though not in stature or degree
Of grouth, untill of perfect age he bee;
So have the faithfull imperfections some,   [650]
Till to a perfect age in Christ they come.

The graces of the Spirit will appeare,
And spring up in his heart thats Sanctifide,
And these the fruits of Righteousnesse will beare
Which in his conversacion are discride,

28

These graces hath he that is Sanctifide,
A detestacion of inniquity,
And love to goodnesse, Zeale and Purity,

Whereof Repentance blessedly proceeds,
Which is endeavour, purpose or intent   [660]
To leave all sin which causefull sorrows breeds
And not to give allowance or consent
To break Gods Law, or least Commandement:
But ever walk exactly there-unto,
Though to the flesh it seemes too much to doe.

So that continuall combates will arise,
Between Gods image, on the soul renewde,
And Sathans image, greatest contraries
Which ever seek each other to exclude,
Though in the end the worst shall be subdude: [670]
Yet in this life it wil in no wise yeeld;
Against whose force, Faith is the only sheild.

Now when a man hath got the victory,
In such a conflict or extream temptacion
He sees Gods love to him abundantly,
By reason of his speciall conservacion,
Which of his favour is a demonstracion;
Now this increaseth peace of conscience most
Together with joy in the Holy-Ghost.

But if the wicked do so far prevaile,   [680]
By Gods permission by some provocacion
To over-come the faithfull being fraile,
And subject to be snar'd with temptacion
When not suspecting such abominacion;
But this their fall is through infirmity
Who shall not be forsaken utterly.

For soon a Godly sorrow will arise
And over-flow the heart of such a one,
Which blessedly the same so mollifies,
That it relents for haveing so mis-gone [690]
Which godly griefe or sorrow is all one
For haveing so displeased God by sinne,
Who hath to him a loveing Father been.

Yea he for this abhors himselfe as vile
Acknowledging his execrable case,
Till he be reconcil'd to God, that while
Himselfe by lowest thoughts he doth abase,
As far unworthy to find any grace;
Yet cries to God in this humiliacion
For the return of wonted consolacion. [700]

And when he hath attain'd recovery,
The breach without delay he fortifies
With stronger resolucion manfully,
And with a Watch impregnable likewise,
Against assaults of this his enimies,
And all assaies of their re-entery
Through which so many perish finally.

This much touching the ground of Truth I hold,
Which sith at first they rectified my mind,
I will not cast them off, as worn and old, [710]
Nor will be so alone to them confind
As not admit of things of higher kind;
But will as God shall light dispence to mee,
(By ayd divine) walk up to each degree.

A Song expressing their happinesse who have Communion with Christ.

Hen scorched with distracting care,
   My mind findes out a shade
Which fruitlesse Trees, false fear, dispair
   And melancoly made,
Where neither bird did sing
   Nor fragrant flowers spring,
Nor any plant of use:
   No sound of happynesse,
Had there at all ingresse,
   Such comforts to produce,   [10]
But *Sorrow* there frequents,
   The Nurce of Discontents,
And *Murmering* her Mayd
   Whose harsh unpleasant noise
All mentall fruits destroyes
   Whereby delight's convayd.

Whereof my judgment being certifide
   My mind from thence did move,
For her concepcion so to provide,
   That it might not abortive prove,   [20]
Which fruit to signifie
   It was conceaved by
Most true intelligence
   Of this sweet truth divine
Who formed thee is thine,   Esay. 54.5.
   Whence sprang this inference;
He too, thats Lord of all
   Will thee beloved call,
Though all else prove unkind;
   Then chearfull may I sing   [30]
Sith I enjoy the Spring,
   Though Sesterns dry I find.

For in our Vnion with the Lord alone,
    Consists our happinesse,
Certainly such who are with Christ at one
    He leaves not comfortlesse,
But come to them he will
    Their Souls with joy to fill,
And them to Fortifie
    Their works to undergo   [40]
And beare their Crosse also,
    With much alacrity:
Who his assisting grace
    Do feelingly imbrace,
With confidence may say,
    Through Christ that strengthens me
No thing so hard I see   *Phil* 4.14
    But what perform I may.

But when the Soul no help can see
    Through sins interposicion,   [50]
Then quite forlorn that while is she,
    Bewailing her condicion;
In which deplored case
    Now such a Soul hath space,
To think how she delayd
    Her Saviour to admit
Who shu'd to her for it,
    And to this purpose sayd,
Open to me my Love,
    My Sister, and my Dove,   *Can.* 5.
My Locks with dew wet are   [61]
    Yet she remissive grew,
Till he himselfe with-drew
    Before she was aware.

But tasting once how sweet he is,
    And smelling his perfumes,

Long can she not his presence misse,
    But griefe her strainth consumes:
For when he visits one
    He cometh not alone,   [70]
But brings abundant grace
    True Light, and Holynesse
And Spirit to expresse
    Ones wants in every case;
For as he wisedome is,
    So is he unto his
Wisedome and Purity,   1 Cor. 1.30
    Which when he seemes to hide,
The soul missing her guide,
    Must needs confused lie.   [80]

Then let them know, that would enjoy
    The firme fruition,
Of his Sweet presence, he will stay
    With single hearts alone,
Who [Lust] their former mate,
    Doe quite exterminate:
With all things that defile
    They that are Christs, truly,
The Flesh do Crucifie
    With its affections vile   *Gal. 5.*
Then grounds of truth are sought   [91]
    New Principles are wrought
Of grace and holinesse,
    Which plantings of the heart
Will spring in every part,
    And so it selfe expresse.

Then shall the Soul like morning bright
    Vnto her Lord appeare,   *Can. 6.10.*
And as the Moone when full of Light
    So fayr is she and cleare,   [100]

33

With that inherent grace
    Thats darted from the Face
Of Christ, that Sunne divine,
    Which hath a purging power
Corruption to devour,
    And Conscience to refine;
Perfection thus begun
    As pure as the Sunne,
The Soul shall be likewise
    With that great Blessednesse,   [110]
Imputed Righteoussenesse
    Which freely Justifies.

They that are thus compleat with Grace
    And know that they are so,
For Glory must set Sayle apace
    Whilst wind doth fitly blow,
Now is the tide of Love,
    Now doth the Angell move;
If that there be defect
    That Soul which sin doth wound,   [120]
Here now is healing found,
    If she no time neglect;
To whom shall be reveald
    What erst hath been conceald,
When brought unto that Light,
    Which in the Soul doth shine
When he thats most divine,
    Declares his presence bright.

Then he will his beloved shew
    The reason wherefore she   [130]
Is seated in a place so low,
    Not from all troubles free;
And wherefore they do thrive
    That wicked works contrive;

Christ telleth his also
   For who as friends he takes
He of his Councell makes,
   And they shall secrets know: *Iohn* 15.15
Such need not pine with cares
   Seeing all things are theirs,   [140]
If they are Christs indeed;   *Cor.* 3.21.
   Therefore let such confesse
They are not comfortlesse,
   Nor left in time of Need.

A Song shewing the Mercies of God to his
people, by interlacing cordiall Com-
forts with fatherly Chastisments.

A S in the time of Winter
   The Earth doth fruitlesse and barren lie,
Till the Sun his course doth run
Through Aries, Taurus, Gemini;
Then he repayres what Cold did decay,
Drawing superfluous moistures away,
And by his luster, together with showers,
The Earth becoms fruitful & plesant with flowers
That what in winter seemed dead,
There by the Sun is life discovered.   [10]

So though that in the Winter
Of sharp Afflictions, fruits seem to dy,
And for that space, the life of Grace
Remayneth in the Root only;
Yet when the Son of Righteousnesse clear
Shall make Summer with us, our spirits to chear,
Warming our hearts with the sense of his favour,

35

Then must our flowers of piety savour,
And then the fruits of righteousnesse
We to the glory of God must expresse. [20]

And as when Night is passed,
The Sun ascending our Hemisphear,
Ill fumes devouers, and opes the powers
Which in our bodies are, and there
He drawes out the spirits of moving and sence
As from the center, to the circumference;
So that the exterior parts are delighted,
And unto mocion and action excited,
And hence it is that with more delight
We undergo labor by day then by night. [30]

So though a Night of Sorrows
May stay proceedings in piety
Yet shall our light like morning bright
Arise out of obscurity,
Then when the Sun that never declines
Shall open the faculties of our mindes,
Stirring up in them that spirituall mocion
Whereby we make towards God with devocion
When kindled by his influence
Our Sacrifice is as pleasing incense. [40]

Now when we feel Gods favour
And the communion with him we have,
Alone we may admit of joy
As having found what most we crave,
Store must we gather while such gleams do last
Against our tryalls sharp winterly blasts
So dispairacion shall swallow us never,
Who know where God once loves, there he loves ever
Though sence of it oft wanting is
Yet still Gods mercies continue with his. [50]

So soon as we discover
Our souls benummed in such a case,
We may not stay, without delay
We must approach the Throne of Grace,
First taking words to our selves to declare
How dead to goodnesse by nature we are,
Then seeking by him who for us did merit
To be enliv'd by his quickening Spirit,
Whose flame doth light our Spark of Grace,
Whereby we may behold his pleased face.   [60]

From whence come beams of comfort,
The chiefest matter of tru Content,
Who tast and see, how sweet they be,
Perceive they are most excellent,
Being a glimce of his presence so bright,
Who dwelleth in unapproachable light:
Whoso hath happily this mercy attayned,
Earnest of blessednesse endlesse hath gayned,
Where happinesse doth not decay
There Spring is eternall, and endlesse is day.   [70]

A Song declaring that a Christian may finde tru Love only where tru Grace is.

NO Knot of Friendship long can hold
   Save that which Grace hath ty'd,
For other causes prove but cold
   When their effects are try'd;
For God who loveth unity
   Doth cause the onely union,
Which makes them of one Family
   Of one mind and communion.

Commocions will be in that place,
    Where are such contraries, [10]
As is inniquity and grace,
    The greatest enimies,
Whom sin doth rule shee doth command
    To hold stiff opposicion
Gainst grace and all the faithfull band
    Which are in her tuision.

This is the cause of home debates,
    And much domestick woes,
That one may find his houshold mates
    To be his greatest foes, [20]
That with the Wolfe the Lamb may bide
    As free from molestacion,
As Saints with sinners, who reside
    In the same habitacion.

By reason of the Enmity
    Between the womans Seed
And mans infernall enimy,
    The Serpent and his breed,
The link of consanguinity
    Could hold true freindship never, [30]
Neither hath neare affinity
    United freinds for ever.

For scoffing *Ishmael* will scorn
    His onely true born brother:
Rebeckahs sonns together born
    Contend with one another,
No bond of nature is so strong
    To cause their hearts to tarry
In unity, who do belong
    To masters so contrary. [40]

The wicked ordinarily
    Gods dearest children hate,
And therfore seek (though groundlesly)
    Their credits to abate,
And though their words and works do show
    No colour of offences
Yet are their hearts most (they trow)
    For all their good pretences.

And those that strongest grace attain,
    Whereby sin is vanquished,   [50]
By Sathan and his cursed train
    Are most contraried;
Because by such the Serpent feeles,
    His head to be most bruised,
He turnes and catches at their heeles,
    By whom he is so used.

His agents he doth instigate,
    To vex, oppose, and fret,
To slander and calumniate,
    Those that have scap't his net,   [60]
Who servants are so diligent,
    That like to *Kain* their father
They whose works are most excellent
    They mischiefe will the rather.

Yet there are of the gracelesse crew
    Who for some private ends
Have sided with prefessors tru
    As truly pious friends,
But to the times of worldly peace
    Their friendship was confined   [70]
Which when some crosses caus'd to cease
    The thred of league untwined.

Such friends unto the *Swallow* may
    Be fitly likened,
Who all the plesant Summer stay
    But are in Winter fled:
They cannot 'bide their freind to see,
    In any kind of trouble,
So pittyfull (forsooth) they bee
    That have the art to double.   [80]

Such will be any thing for one
    Who hath of nothing need,
Their freindship stands in word alone,
    And none at all in deed,
How open mouth'd so e're they are,
    They bee as closely handed,
Who will (they know) their service spare,
    They're his to be commanded.

Therefore let no true hearted one
    Releife at need expect,   [90]
From opposits to vertue known,
    Who can him not afect:
For his internall ornaments,
    Will ever lovely make him
Though all things pleasing outward sence
    Should utterly forsake him.

In choise of Freinds let such therefore
    Prefer the godly wise,
To whom he may impart the store
    That in his bosome lies: [100]
And let him not perniciously
    Communicate his favours,
To all alike indifferently,
    Which shewes a mind that wavers.

Gods children to each other should
    Most open hearted bee;
Who by the same precepts are rul'd,
    And in one Faith agree,
Who shall in true felicity,
    Where nothing shall offend them   [110]
Together dwell eternally,
    To which I do commend them.

A Song demonstrating
The vanities of Earthly things.

S Hall Sadnesse perswade me never to sing
  But leave unto Syrens that excellent thing,
No that may not be, for truely I find,
The sanguin complexion to mirth is enclin'd.

Moreover, they may who righteousnesse love,
Be soberly merry, and sorrows remove,
They only have right to rejoycing allwaies
Whose joy may be mixed with prayer and praise.

Wherefore rejoyceth the epicure?
As though his fadeing delights would endure,   [10]
Whereas they are ended, as soon as begun,
For all things are vanity under the Sun.

Riches and Honour, Fame and Promocion,
Idols, to whom the most do their devocion;
How fadeing they are, I need not to show,
For this by experience, too many doe know.

They that delight in costly attire,
If they can compasse the things they desire,

Have onely obtained, what sin first procured,
And many to folly are therby alured.   [20]

Learning is sure an excellent thing,
From whence all Arts and Sciences spring,
Yet it is not from vanity free,
For many great Scholars prophane often be.

Whoso hath studied Geometry,
Or gained experience in Geography,
By tedious labour much knowledg may gain,
Yet in the conclusion, hee'l find all is vain.

He that hath studied Astronomy,
Though his meditacion ascend to the Sky   [30]
He may mis of heaven and heavenly blis,
If that he can practise no studdy but this,

But they that delight in Divinity,
And to be exquisit in Theology,
Much heavenly comfort in this life may gain,
And when it is ended their joyes shall remain.

What should I speak more of vanities,
To use many words when few may suffice,
It argueth folly, therfore I have don,
Concluding, all's vanity under the Sun.   [40]

A Song manifesting
The Saints eternall Happinesse

SOund is the Minde
     Which doth that Hope possesse
Whose object is Eternall joy

42

Or Heavens Happinesse;
Such healthfull hearts
    Their spirits doe sustain,
In thinking on the Rest which for
    Gods peeple doth remain,
A Treasure inaccessible,
    Or Everlasting Life,   [10]
A blessed State which never shall
    be cumbered with strife   *Heb. 4.6*

Salvacion
    With endlesse Glory cleare,   *2 Tim. 2.10*
And each good thing to be desir'd
    Are in their Fountain there;
Flowers are here,
    Together with the weeds
Exposed to all kinde of stormes,
    Which much confusion breeds: [20]
Some for weaknesse are dismaid,
    And some are comfortlesse,
Because of some defect of sence,
    Or want of comlinesse.

Grant some may have
    Proporcion so compleat,
That correspondency of parts
    Declares Perfections seat
Yet doubtles such
    Their burthen have also   [30]
By reason of their travell which
    They needs must undergo,
For in every calling is
    A tedious wearinesse
Which whoso followes carefully
    Is driven to confesse

Further suppose
   One might be freed from all
Afflictions which externall are,
   Or crosses corporall   [40]
Yet if the soule
   Be sencible of sin
It cannot be but such will have
   Enough to do within:
For to Preserve the heart and waies
   From being over grown
With fruits of that contagious seed
   That's in our nature sown.

Doubting some times
   The Soul with anguish tires,   [50]
Who must anon encounter with
   inordinate desires:
Lust oft prevailes,
   And then the consequence,
Will be a great ecclips of grace,
   And losse of comfort sence,
In striving to recover peace,
   The soule is oft opprest,
As he that's conscious of his sin,
   Hath here but little rest.   [60]

From all those woes
   And many more that bee,
The Saint that finisht hath his course
   Shall be for ever free,
And likewise have
   For ever to posesse
A most exquisit Diadem,
   The Crown of righteousnesse,   2. Tim. 4.8.
Of that divine inheritance
   Which fadeth not away,   1. Pet. 1.5.

They shall be really posest,   [71]
   And ever it enjoy.

Bodies which here
   Are matter thick and grosse,
Attaining to this happinesse,
   Are freed from their drosse:
And as the Sunn
   Appeares in brightest Sky,   *Mat.* 13.43.
So every body glorifi'd
   Shall be for clarity,   [80]
And likewise be impassible,
   Uncapable of pain
Having agility to move,
   Whose vigour shall remain.

Glorified Soules,
   Are fild with all delight,
Because the spring of Beuty is
   The object of their sight:
Also they have,
   (Their joy to amplify)   [90]
Immediat sweet communion with
   The blessed Trinity.
Which satisfies the appetite,
   Which else were empty still,
Because no finite comfort can
   Content the mind and will.

Briefly a word
   Of place and company
Which Saints in Glory shall enioy,
   The place is heavenly   *Heb.* 12.
Ierusalem,   [101]
   The citty of the Lord:
Discover'd by such precious things   *Rev.* 21.

As pleasure most afford,
The consorts, Angells numberlesse,
   The whole Assembly   *Heb.* 12.
Of Saints, who shall for ever dwell
   With Christ Eternally.

Why hath the Lord
   For his, such Ioyes prepar'd   [110]
Because their pacient sufferings
   He richly will reward,
This light distresse   *2 Cor.* 4.17
   Which for a moment dures
An excellent eternall waight
   Of Glory his procures,
But our afflictions merit not   *Rom.* 8.18.
   This Glory that exceeds
But it, as Gods all other gifts,
   Of his free-Love proceeds.   *Rom.* 6.23.

Now they that have   [121]
   This Hope of Heaven sure,
Shew it by striving to be cleane
   As Christ our Lord is pure,   *1 Iohn:* 3.3.
Also they take
   Their croses chearfully
Because a substance they expect,
   Eternall heavenly,   *Heb.* 10.34.
To which my Soule aspired still
   And cannot setled be,   [130]
Till shee returns againe to him
   That gave her unto me.   *Ecl.* 12.7.

A Song exciting to spirituall Alacrity.

Discomforts will the heart contract
    And joy will cause it to dilate;
That every part its part may act,
    A heart enlarg'd must animate.

Unfruitfull ones therfore they are
    That planted be in sorrow's shade,
Sith by the blasts of cloudy care
    They are unfit for action made.

The ill effects of fruitlesse greife
    Are in this place no further shown,   [10]
Because the meanes of true releife
    Is more convenient to be known.

Now he in whom all fullnesse dwels   *Col.* 1.9.
    All good and meanes of good must bee,
His presence Sathans rule expells
    And doth from Legall terror free.   *Gal.* 3.13.

So that their Soules which are so blessed
    His sacred presence to enioy,
Can never be so much distressed
    But consolacion find they may.   [20]

Having a hiding place secure,   *Isay.* 32.1.2
    And covert from the stormy wind,
And streames of water perfect pure
    To vivify and cheare the mind.

If scorched with afflictions heat
    They to their shady rock may fly,
And be in safties bosome seat
    And lap of true felicity.

47

Where are delights Angelicall,
    The quintisence of all good things,   [30]
Refined wine to cheare withall
    And food which life eternall brings.

Which though the Saints by faith posesse,
    Doe not suppose it solace give,
But truly reall happinesse,
    As they that feele alone beleeve.

Who thence abundant strength collect,
    In all condicions to support,
Nor troubles can them much deject,
    Who have this soules defensive Fort.   [40]

Suppose temptacion sist them sore,
    Sufficient grace will them releive,   2 Cor. 12.9.
And make their Faith appeare the more,
    Which will to them the Conquest give.

Or be their Scourge some outward Crosse,
    As causlesse hate, or poverty,
Decay of parts, disease, or losse
    Of Credit, Freinds, or Liberty.

Nay were their state compos'd of woes,
    In whom the Morning Star doth shine,   [50]
Whose lively luster will disclose,
    To his a heritage divine,

Which he of Love did them procure,
    With freedom, not to *Adam* dain'd
To tast the Tree of Life most pure,
    Whereby the soule alone's sustain'd

The sence of Love-Eternall, doth,
    with Love, Obedience still produce,

Which active is, and passive both,
    So suffrings are of speciall use.   [60]

Bearing the soule with joy and peace,
    Through true beleeving, evermore,
Whose sweet contentments take encrease,
    From heavens never-fayling store.

Another Song exciting to spiri-
tuall Mirth.

THe Winter being over
    In order comes the Spring,
Which doth green Hearbs discover
And cause the Birds to sing;
The Night also expired,
Then comes the Morning bright,
Which is so much desired
By all that love the Light;
This may learn
Them that mourn   [10]
To put their Griefe to flight.
The Spring succeedeth Winter,
And Day must follow Night.

He therefore that sustaineth
Affliction or Distresse,
Which ev'ry member paineth,
And findeth no relesse;
Let such therefore despaire not,
But on firm Hope depend
Whose Griefes immortall are not,   [20]
And therefore must have end:
They that faint

With complaint
Therefore are too blame,
They ad to their afflictions,
And amplify the same.

For if they could with patience
A while posesse the minde,
By inward Consolacions
They might refreshing find,   [30]
To sweeten all their Crosses
That little time they 'dure;
So might they gain by losses,
And sharp would sweet procure;
But if the minde
Be inclinde
To Vnquietnesse
That only may be called
The worst of all Distresse.

He that is melancolly   [40]
Detesting all Delight,
His Wits by sottish Folly
Are ruinated quite;
Sad Discontent and Murmors
To him are insident,
Were he posest of Honors,
He could not be content:
Sparks of joy
Fly away,
Floods of Cares arise,   [50]
And all delightfull Mocions
In the conception dies.

But those that are contented
However things doe fall,
Much Anguish is prevented,

And they soon freed from all;
They finish all their Labours
With much felicity,
Theyr joy in Troubles savours
Of perfect Piety,   [60]
Chearfulnesse
Doth expresse
A setled pious minde
Which is not prone to grudging
From murmoring refinde.

Lascivious joy I prayse not,
Neither do it allow,
For where the same decayes not
No branch of peace can grow;
For why, it is sinister   [70]
As is excessive Griefe,
And doth the Heart sequester
From all good: to be briefe,
Vain Delight
Passeth quite
The bounds of modesty,
And makes one apt to nothing
But sensuality.

This Song sheweth that God is the strength
of his People, whence they have
support and comfort.

MY straying thoughts, reduced stay,
And so a while retired,
Such observacions to survay
Which memory hath registred,
That were not in oblivion dead.

51

In which reveiw of mentall store,
One note affordeth comforts best,
Cheifly to be preferd therfore,
As in a Cabinet or Chest
One jewell may exceed the rest.   [10]

God is the Rock of his Elect
In whom his grace is incoate,
This note, my soule did most affect,
It doth such power intimate
To comfort and corroberate.

God is a Rock first in respect
He shadows his from hurtfull heat,
Then in regard he doth protect
His servants still from dangers great
And so their enimies defeat.   [20]

In some dry desart Lands (they say)
Are mighty Rocks, which shadow make
Where passengers that go that way,
May rest, and so refreshing take,
Their sweltish Wearinesse to slake.

So in this world such violent
Occasions, find we still to mourn,
That scorching heat of Discontent
Would all into combustion turn
And soon our soules with anguish burn,   [30]

Did not our Rock preserve us still,
Whose Spirit, ours animates,
That wind that bloweth where it will   *Iohn.* 3.8
Sweetly our soules refrigerates,
And so distructive heat abates.

From this our Rock proceeds likewise,
Those living streames, which graciously
Releives the soule which scorched lies,
Through sence of Gods displeasure high,
Due to her for inniquity.   [40]

So this our Rock refreshing yeelds,
To those that unto him adhere,
Whom likewise mightily he sheilds,
So that they need not faint nor fear
Though all the world against them were.

Because he is their strength and tower,
Whose power none can equalize,
Which onely gives the use of power
Which justly he to them denies,
Who would against his servants rise.   [50]

Not by selfe power nor by might,
But by Gods spirit certainly,   *Zach.* 4.
Men compasse and attain their right,
For what art thou, O mountain high!
Thou shalt with valleys, even ly.

Happy was *Israell,* and why,
Jehovah was his Rock alone,   *Deu.* 33.29.
The *Sword of his Excellency,*
His sheild of Glory mighty known,
In saving those that are his own.   [60]

Experience of all ages shewes,
That such could never be dismayd
Who did by Faith on God repose,
Confessing him their onely ayd,
Such were alone in safty stayd.

One may have freinds, who have a will
To further his felicity,
And yet be wanting to him still,
Because of imbecility,
In power and ability.   [70]

But whom the Lord is pleas'd to save,
Such he is able to defend,
His grace and might no limmits have,
And therefore can to all extend
Who doe or shall on him depend.

Nor stands he therefore surely,
Whose Freinds most powerfull appeare,
Because of mutabillity
To which all mortalls subject are,
Whose favours run now here, now there.   [80]

But in our Rock and mighty Fort,
Of change no shadow doth remain,
His favours he doth not Transport
As trifles movable and vain,
His Love alone is lasting gain.

Therfore my soule do thou depend,
Upon that Rock which will not move,
When all created help shall end
Thy Rock impregnable will prove,
Whom still embrace with ardent Love.   [90]

Another Song.

THe Winter of my infancy being over-past
I then supposed, suddenly the Spring would hast
Which useth every thing to cheare
With invitacion to recreacion
This time of yeare,

The Sun sends forth his radient beames to warm the ground
The drops distil, between the gleams delights abound,
Ver brings her mate the flowery Queen,
The Groves shee dresses, her Art expresses
On every Green.   [10]

But in my Spring it was not so, but contrary,
For no delightfull flowers grew to please the eye,
No hopefull bud, nor fruitfull bough,
No moderat showers which causeth flowers
To spring and grow.

My Aprill was exceeding dry, therfore unkind;
Whence tis that small utility I look to find,
For when that Aprill is so dry,
(As hath been spoken) it doth betoken
Much scarcity.   [20]

Thus is my Spring now almost past in heavinesse
The Sky of pleasure's over-cast with sad distresse
For by a comfortlesse Eclips,
Disconsolacion and sore vexacion,
My blossom nips.

Yet as a garden is my mind enclosed fast
Being to safety so confind from storm and blast
Apt to produce a fruit most rare,

That is not common with every woman
That fruitfull are.   [30]

A Love of goodnesse is the cheifest plant therin
The second is, (for to be briefe) Dislike to sin,
These grow in spight of misery,
Which Grace doth nourish and cause to flourish
Continually.

But evill mocions, currupt seeds, fall here also
whenc springs prophanesse as do weeds where flowers grow
Which must supplanted be with speed
These weeds of Error, Distrust and Terror,
Lest woe succeed   [40]

So shall they not molest, the plants before exprest
Which countervails these outward wants, & purchase rest
Which more commodious is for me
Then outward pleasures or earthly treasures
Enjoyd would be.

My little Hopes of worldly Gain I fret not at,
As yet I do this Hope retain; though Spring be lat
Perhaps my Sommer-age may be,
Not prejudiciall, but benificiall
Enough for me.   [50]

Admit the worst it be not so, but stormy too,
Ile learn my selfe to undergo more then I doe
And still content my self with this
Sweet Meditacion and Contemplacion
Of heavenly blis,

Which for the Saints reserved is, who persevere
In Piety and Holynesse, and godly Feare,
The pleasures of which blis divine

56

Neither Logician nor Rhetorician
Can well define.   [60]
                            Finis

Another Song.

Having restrained Discontent,
The onely Foe to Health and Witt,
I sought by all meanes to prevent
The causes which did nourish it,
Knowing that they who are judicious
Have alwaies held it most pernicious.

Looking to outward things, I found
Not that which Sorrow might abate,
But rather cause them to abound
Then any Greife to mitigate   [10]
Which made me seek by supplicacion
Internall Peace and Consolacion

Calling to mind their wretchednesse
That seem to be in happy case
Having externall happinesse
But therewithall no inward grace;
Nor are their minds with knowledg pollisht
In such all vertues are abollisht

For where the mind's obscure and dark
There is no vertu resident,   [20]
Of goodnesse there remaines no spark;
Distrustfullnesse doth there frequent
For Ignorance the cause of error
May also be the cause of terror

As doth the Sun-beames beutify
The Sky, which else doth dim appeare

So Knowldg doth exquisitly
The Mind adorn, delight and cleare
Which otherwise is most obscure,
Full of enormities impure.   [30]

So that their Soules polluted are
That live in blockish Ignorance,
Which doth their miseries declare
And argues plainly that their wants
More hurtfull are then outward Crosses
Infirmities, Reproach, or Losses.

Where saving Knowledg doth abide,
The peace of Conscience also dwels
And many Vertues more beside
Which all obsurdities expels,   [40]
And fils the Soule with joy Celestiall
That shee regards not things Terrestiall.

Sith then the Graces of the Mind
Exceeds all outward Happinesse,
What sweet Contentment do they find
Who are admitted to possesse
Such matchlesse Pearles, so may we call them:
For Precious is the least of all them.

Which when I well considered
My greife for outward crosses ceast,   [50]
Being not much discouraged
Although afflictions still encreast,
Knowing right well that tribulacion
No token is of Reprobacion.

58

Another Song.

EXcessive worldly Greife the Soule devouers
And spoyles the activnesse of all the Powers,
Through indisposing them to exercise
What should demonstrate their abilities,
By practicall improvment of the same
Unto the Glory of the givers name.
Though Envy wait to blast the Blossoms green
Of any Vertu soon as they are seen,
Yet none may therfore just occasion take
To shun what Vertu manifest should make,   [10]
For like the Sun shall Vertu be beheld
When Clouds of Envy shall be quite dispeld;
Though there be some of no disart at all
Who no degree in worth can lower fall,
Prefer'd before the Verteous whom they taunt
Onely because of some apparent want,
Which is as if a Weed without defect
Before the Damask Rose should have respect,
Because the Rose a leafe or two hath lost,
And this the Weed of all his parts can boast;   [20]
Or elce as if a monstrous Clout should be
Prefer'd before the purest Lawn to see,
Because the Lawn hath spots and this the Clout
Is equally polluted thoroughout
Therefore let such whose vertu favours merits,
Shew their divinly magnanimious spirits
By disregarding such their approbacion
Who have the worthlesse most in estimacion,
For who loves God above all things, not one
Who understands not that in him alone   [30]
All causes that may move affections are,
Glimpses wherof his creatures doe declare,
This being so, who can be troubled

59

When as his gifts are undervalued,
Seeing the giver of all things likewise
For want of knowledg many underprise.

A Song composed in time of the Civill Warr, when the wicked did much insult over the godly.

With *Sibells* I cannot Devine
  Of future things to treat,
Nor with *Parnassus* Virgins Nine
  Compose in Poëms neat
Such mentall mocions which are free
  Concepcions of the mind,
Which notwithstanding will not be
  To thoughts alone confind.

With *Deborah* twere joy to sing
  When that the Land hath Rest,   [10]
And when that Truth shall freshly spring,
  Which seemeth now deceast,
But some may waiting for the same
  Go on in expectacion
Till quick conceipt be out of frame,
  Or till Lifes expiracion.

Therefore who can, and will not speak
  Betimes in Truths defence,
Seeing her Foes their malice wreak,
  And some with smooth pretence   [20]
And colours which although they glose
  Yet being not ingraind,
In time they shall their luster lose
  As cloth most foully staind.

60

See how the Foes of Truth devise
    Her followers to defame.
First by Aspersions false and Lies
    To kill them in good Name;
Yet here they will in no wise cease
    But Sathans course they take   [30]
To spoyl their Goods and Wealths increase,
    And so at Life they make.

Such with the Devill further go
    The Soule to circumvent
In that they seeds of Error sow
    And to false Worships tempt,
And Scriptures falsly they apply
    Their Errors to maintain,
Opposing Truth implicitly
    The greater side to gain.   [40]

And to bind Soul and Body both
    To Sathans service sure
Therto they many ty by Oath,
    Or cause them to endure
The Losse of lightsom Liberty
    And suffer Confiscacion,
A multitude they force therby
    To hazard their Salvacion.

Another sort of Enimies
    To Lady Verity,   [50]
Are such who no Religion prise,
    But Carnall Liberty
Is that for which they do contest
    And venture Life and State,
Spurning at all good meanes exprest,
    The force of Vice to bate.

61

Yet these are they, as some conceit,
   Who must again reduce,
And all things set in order strait
   Disjoynted by abuse,   [60]
And wakeing witts may think no lesse
   If Fiends and Furies fell,
May be suppos'd to have successe
   Disorders to expell.

How-ever Truth to fade appeare,
   Yet can shee never fall,
Her Freinds have no abiding here,
   And may seem wasted all;
Yet shall a holy Seed remain
   The Truth to vindicate,   [70]
Who will the wrongeds Right regain
   And Order elevate.

What time Promocion, Wealth, and Peace,
   The Owners shall enjoy,
Whose Light shall as the Sun encrease
   Unto the perfect Day
Then shall the Earth with blessings flow,
   And Knowledg shall abound.
The *Cause* that's now derided so,
   Shall then most just be found.   [80]

Prophanesse must be fully grown,
   And such as it defend
Must be ruind or overthrown,
   And to their place desend,
The Sonns of strife their force must cease,
   Having fulfild their crime,
And then the Son of wished peace
   Our Horizon will clime.

That there are such auspicious dayes
    To come, we may not doubt,   [90]
Because the Gospels splendant rayes
    Must shine the World throughout:
By Jewes the Faith shall be embrac't
    The Man of Sin must fall,
New Babell shall be quite defac't
    With her devices all.

Then Truth will spread and high appeare,
    As grain when weeds are gon,
Which may the Saints afflicted cheare
    Oft thinking hereupon;   [100]
Sith they have union with that sort
    To whom all good is ty'd
They can in no wise want support
    Though most severely try'd.

Another Song.

Time past we understood by story
    The strength of Sin a Land to waste,
Now God to manifest his Glory
The truth hereof did let us taste,
For many years, this Land appears
Of usefull things the Nursery,
Refresht and fenc'd with unity.

But that which crown'd each other Blessing
Was evidence of Truth Divine,
The Word of Grace such Light expressing,   [10]
Which in some prudent Hearts did shine,
Whose Flame inclines those noble minds
To stop the Course of Prophanacion
And so make way for Reformacion.

But He that watcheth to devour,
This their intent did soon discry,
For which he strait improves his power
This worthy work to nullify
With Sophistry and Tiranny,
His agents he forthwith did fill   [20]
Who gladly execute his will.

And first they prove by Elocution
And Hellish Logick to traduce
Those that would put in execucion,
Restraint of every known abuse;
They seperate and 'sturb the State,
And would all Order overthrow,
The better sort were charged so.

Such false Reports did fill all places,
Corrupting some of each degree,   [30]
He whom the highest Title graces
From hearing slanders was not free,
Which Scruple bred, and put the Head
With primest members so at bate
Which did the Body dislocate.

A Lying Spirit mis-informed
The common-peeple, who suppose
If things went on to be reformed
They should their ancient Customs lose,
And be beside to courses ty'd   [40]
Which they nor yet their Fathers knew,
And so be wrapt in fangles new.

Great multitudes therefore were joyned
To Sathans plyant instruments,
With mallice, ignorance combined,
And both at Truth their fury vents;

First Piety as Enimy
They persecute, oppose, revile,
Then Freind as well as Foe they spoyle.

The beuty of the Land's abollisht,   [50]
With Fabericks by Art contriv'd,
The many of them quite demollisht,
And many of their homes depriv'd
Some mourn for freinds untimely ends,
And some for necessaries faint,
With which they parted by constraint.

But from those storms hath God preserved
A people to record his praise,
Who sith they were therefore reserved
Must to the heigth their Spirits raise   [60]
To magnify his lenity,
Who safely brought them through the fire
To let them see their hearts desire

Which many faithfull ones deceased
With teares desired to behold,
Which is the Light of Truth professed
Without obscuring shaddowes old,
When spirits free, not tyed shall be
To frozen Forms long since compos'd,
When lesser knowledg was disclos'd.   [70]

Who are preserv'd from foes outragious,
Noteing the Lords unfound-out wayes,
Should strive to leave to after-ages
Some memorandums of his praise,
That others may admiring say
Unsearchable his judgments are,
As do his works alwayes declare.

Meditacions

The first Meditacion.

THe Morning is at hand, my Soule awake,
Rise from the sleep of dull security;
Now is the time, anon 't will be to late,
Now hast thou golden opportunity
For to behold thy naturall estate
And to repent and be regenerate.

Delay no longer though the Flesh thee tell,
Tis time enough hereafter to repent,
Strive earnestly such mocions to expell,
Remember this thy courage to augment   [10]
The first fruits God requir'd for sacrifice,
The later he esteemed of no price.

First let's behold our natural estate
How dangerous and damnable it is,
And thereupon grow to exceeding hate
With that which is the onely cause of this;
The which is Sin, yea Disobedience
Even that which was our first parents offence.

The reasonable Soule undoubtedly
Created was at first free from offence,   [20]
In Wisdom, Holinesse, and Purity,

66

It did resemble the Divine Essence,
Which being lost, the Soule of man became
Like to the Serpent, causer of the same.

The Understanding, Will, Affections cleare,
Each part of Soule and Body instantly
Losing their purity, corrupted were
Throughout as by a loathsom Leprocy
The rayes of Vertu were extinguisht quite
And Vice usurpeth rule with force and might.   [30]

This sudden change from sanctitude to sin
Could but prognosticat a fearfull end,
Immediatly the dollour did begin,
The Curse that was pronounc'd, none might defend,
Which Curse is in this life a part or some,
The fulnesse thereof in the life to come.

The Curse that to the Body common is
The sence of Hunger, Thirst, of Sicknes, Pain:
The Soules Callamities exceedeth this,
A Tast of Hell shee often doth sustain,   [40]
Rebukes of Conscience, threatning plagues for sin,
A world of Torment oft shee hath within.

Unlesse the Conscience dead and seared be,
Then runs the soule in errors manifold,
Her danger deep shee can in no wise see,
And therefore unto every sin is bold,
The Conscience sleeps, the Soule is dead in sin,
Nere thinks of Hell untill shee comes therein.

Thus is the Conscience of the Reprobate,
Either accusing unto desperacion,   [50]
Or elce benummed, cannot instigate
Nor put the Soule in mind of reformacion;

Both work for ill unto the castaway,
Though here they spent their time in mirth and play.

Yet can they have no sound contentment here,
In midst of laughter oft the heart is sad:
This world is full of woe & hellish feare
And yeelds forth nothing long to make us glad
As they that in the state of nature dy
Passe but from misery to misery.   [60]

Consider this my soule, yet not despaire,
To comfort thee again let this suffice,
There is a Well of grace, whereto repaire,
First wash away thy foul enormities
With teares proceeding from a contrite heart,
With thy beloved sins thou must depart.

Inordinate affections, and thy Will,
And carnall wisdom, must thou mortify,
For why, they are corrupt, prophane and ill,
And prone to nothing but impiety,   [70]
Yet shalt thou not their nature quite deface,
Their ruines must renewed be by grace.

If that thou canst unfainedly repent,
With hatred therunto thy sins confesse,
And not because thou fearest punishment
But that therby thou didst Gods Laws transgress
Resolving henceforth to be circumspect,
Desiring God to frame thy wayes direct.

Each member of thy body thou dost guide,
Then exercise them in Gods service most   [80]
Let every part be throughly sanctifide
As a meet Temple for the Holy Ghost;

Sin must not in our mortall bodies raign
It must expelled be although with pain

    Thou must not willingly one sin detain,
    For so thou mayst debarred be of blis,
    Grace with inniquity will not remain,
    Twixt Christ and Belial no communion is,
Therefore be careful every sin to fly,
And see thou persevere in piety.   [90]

    So mayst thou be perswaded certainly,
    The Curse shall in no wise endanger thee,
    Although the body suffer misery
    Yet from the second death thou shalt be free;
They that are called here to Holinesse
Are sure elected to eternall blisse.

    A Taste of blessednesse here shalt thou say,
    Thy Conscience shall be at Tranquility,
    And in the Life to com thou shalt enjoy
    The sweet fruicion of the Trinity,   [100]
Society with Saints then shalt thou have,
Which in this life thou didst so often crave.

    Let this then stir thee up to purity,
    Newnesse of life, and speedy Conversion,
    To Holinesse and to integrity,
    Make conscience of impure thoughts unknown
Pray in the Spirit with sweet Contemplacion
Be vigilant for to avoid Temptacion.

The Preamble.

Amid the Oceon of Adversity,
Neare whelmed in the Waves of sore Vexacion,
Tormented with the Floods of Misery,
And almost in the Gulfe of Despairacion,
Neare destitute of Comfort, full of Woes,
This was her Case that did the same compose:

At length Jehovah by his power divine,
This great tempestious Storm did mittigate.
And cause the Son of Righteousnesse to shine
Upon his Child that seemed desolate, [10]
Who was refreshed, and that immediatly,
And Sings as follows with alacrity.

The second Meditacion.

THe Storm of Anguish being over-blown,
   To praise Gods mercies now I may have space,
For that I was not finally orethrown,
   But was supported by his speciall grace;
The Firmament his glory doth declare,   *Psal.* 19.1
Yet over all his works, his mercies are.   *Psal,* 145.9

The Contemplacion of his mercies sweet,
   Hath ravished my Soule with such delight
Who to lament erst while was onely meet,
   Doth now determine to put griefe to flight,   [10]
Being perswaded, hereupon doth rest,
Shee shall not be forsaken though distrest.

Gods Favour toward me is hereby proved,
   For that he hath not quite dejected me;

Why then, though crosses be not yet removed
  Yet so seasoned with pacience they be,
As they excite me unto godlinesse,
The onely way to endlesse happinesse.

  Which earthly muckworms can in no wise know
  Being of the Holy Spirit destitute,   [20]
  They favour onely earthly things below;
  Who shall with them of saving Grace dispute,
Shall find them capable of nothing lesse
Though Christianity they do professe.

  Let *Esaus* porcion fall unto these men,
  The Fatnesse of the Earth let them possesse
  No other thing they can desire then,
  Having no taste of Heavens happinesse,
They care not for Gods Countenance so bright,
Their Corn and Wine and Oyle is their delight.   [30]

  To compasse this and such like is their care,
  But having past the period of their dayes,
  Bereft of all but miseries they are,
  Their sweet delight with mortall life decayes,
But godlinesse is certainly great gain,   1. *Tim.* 6.6
Immortall blisse they have, who it retain.

  They that are godly and regenerate,
  Endu'd with saving Knowledg, Faith, and Love,
  When they a future blisse premeditate,
  It doth all bitter passion quite remove;   [40]
Though oft they feel the want of outward things
Their heavenly meditacions, comfort brings.

  They never can be quite disconsolate,
  Because they have the onely Comforter

Which doth their minds alway illuminate,
   And make them fleshly pleasures much abhorr,
For by their inward light they plainly see
How vain all transitory pleasures bee.

   Moreover, if they be not only voyd
   Of earthly pleasures and commodities,   [50]
   But oftentimes be greivously annoyd
   With sundry kinds of great Calammities,
Whether it be in Body, Goods, or Name,
With pacience they undergo the same.

   And why? because they know and be aware
   That all things work together for the best,
   To them that love the Lord and called are,   *Ro.* 8 28.
   According to his purpose, therefore blest
Doubtlesse they be, his knowledg that obtain,
No Losse may countervail their blessed Gain.   [60]

   Which makes them neither murmor nor repine
   When God is pleasd with Crosses them to try,
   who out of darknesse caused light to shine,   *2 Cor* 4.6.
   Can raise them Comfort out of Misery
They know right well and therefore are content
To beare with pacience any Chastisment.

   This difference is betwixt the good and bad;
   When as for sin the godly scourged are,
   And godly Sorrow moves them to be sad,
   These speeches or the like they will declare: [70]
O will the Lord absent himselfe for ever?
Will he vouchsafe his mercy to me never?

   What is the cause I am afflicted so?
   The cause is evident I do perceive.

My Sins have drawn upon me all this woe,
The which I must confesse and also leave,
Then shall I mercy find undoubtedly,   *Pro.* 28.13.
And otherwise no true prosperity.

Whilst sin hath rule in me, in vain I pray,
Or if my Soule inniquity affects,   [80]
If this be true, as tis, I boldly say,
The prayer of the wicked, God rejects;   *Pro.* 15, 8.
If in my heart I wickednesse regard
How can I hope my prayer shall be heard.   *Psal.* 66

If I repent, here may I Comfort gather,
Though in my prayers there be weaknesse much
Christ siteth at the right hand of his Father
To intercede and make request for such,   *Rom.* 8. 33
Who have attained to sincerity,
Though somthing hindered by infirmity.   [90]

I will forthwith abandon and repent,
Not onely palpable inniquities,
But also all alowance or consent
To sinfull mocions or infirmities;
And when my heart and wayes reformed be,
God will with-hold nothing that's good from me   *Psal.* 84.

So may I with the *Psalmist* truly say,
Tis good for me that I have been afflicted,
Before I troubled was, I went astray,   *Psal.* 119
But now to godlinesse I am adicted;   [100]
If in Gods Lawes I had not took delight,
I in my troubles should have perisht quite.

Such gracious speeches usually proceed
From such a Spirit that is Sanctifide,

Who strives to know his own defects and need
And also seekes to have his wants supplide;
But certainly the wicked do not so
As do their speeches and distempers show.

At every crosse they murmor, vex and fret,
And in their passion often will they say,   [110]
How am I with Calamities beset!
I think they will mee utterly destray,
The cause hereof I can in no wise know
But that the *Destinies* will have it so

Unfortunate am I and quite forlorn,
Oh what disastrous Chance befalleth me!
Vnder some hurtfull Plannet I was born
That will (I think) my Confusion be,
And there are many wickeder then I
Who never knew the like adversity.   [120]

These words do breifly show a carnall mind
Polluted and corrupt with Ignorance,
Where godly Wisdom never yet hath shin'd
For that they talk of *Destiny* or *Chance*;
For if Gods Power never can abate,
He can dispose of that he did create

If God alone the True Almighty be
As we beleive, acknowledg, and confesse,
Then supream Governor likewise is he
Disposing all things, be they more or lesse;   [130]
The eyes of God in every place do see
The good and bad, and what their actions bee.

The thought hereof sufficeth to abate
My heavinesse in great'st extremity,

74

When Grace unto my Soul did intimate
That nothing comes by *Chance* or *Destiny*,
But that my God and Saviour knowes of all
That either hath or shall to me befall

Who can his servants from all troubles free
And would I know my Crosses all prevent,   [140]
But that he knowes them to be good for me
Therefore I am resolv'd to be content,
For though I meet with many Contradictions
Yet Grace doth always sweeten my Afflictions.

The third Meditacion.

FAint not my Soule, but wait thou on the Lord
    Though he a while his answer may suspend,
Yet know (according to his blessed word)
He will vouchsafe refreshing in the end,
Yea though he seem for to withdraw his grace,
And doth not alwaies show his pleasing face.

As by the Sun, though not still shining bright,
We do enjoy no small Commodity,
Whilst that the day is govern'd by his Light,
And other works of Nature testify   [10]
His wonderfull and rare Effects alwayes,
Though often vayled be his shining rayes.

So it is no small mercy, though we see
Gods Countenance not alwaies shining bright,
That by the same our minds enlightned be,
And our affections guided by that Light,
And whilst the winter-fruits as it were we find
In Pacience, Sufferings, and Peace of mind.

Then let it not be told in *Ashkelon*,
Neither in *Gath* let it be published,   [20]
That those that seek the Lord and him alone
In any case should be discouraged,
Lest it rejoyce the wicked this to see,
Who think the wayes of grace unpleasant be.

Where-as they are most pleasant, sweet, and fair
Yeilding delights which onely satisfy
Our minds, which else transported are with care
And restlesse wandrings continually,
But those that do no taste hereof attain
Seek rather for content in pleasures vain.   [30]

When *Kain* had lost the happy harmony,
He by a peace-full Conscience might enjoy
His nephew *Iuball* then most skillfully
Invented Musick, thereby to convey
Unto the outward eare some melody,
But no true joy comes to the heart thereby.

For it is onely a Certificate
Brought by Gods Spirit from the Throne of Grace
That may delight the Soule Regenerate,
Which certifies her of her happy case,   [40]
That shee's already in a gracious state,
Which will in endlesse glory consummate.

Again, the blessed Soule may take delight,
To think on Sions great prosperity,
In that the Gospell long hath shined bright,
Sustaining no Eclips by Heresy,
So that the meanes of knowledg is so free,
Gods Worship rightly may performed be.

If then my Soule, the Lord thy Porcion be
Delight'st his Word and sacred Covenants   [50]
Wherby his Graces are conveyed to thee,
    As Earnests of divine inheritance,
And which may cause tru comfort to abound
Thy Lot is fallen in a pleasant ground,

    Then let not any trouble thee dismay
    Seeing the Light of Grace to thee hath shone
    The sable Weed of Sadnesse lay away,
        And put the Garment of Salvacion on,
With chearfullnesse, Gods blessings entertain
Let not the object of thy mirth be vain,   [60]

    Which as a Cloud would stop the influence
    Of that true Light that doth the Soule refine
    And predisposeth it through lively sence
        To that eternall brightnesse most divine;
Then chiefly to admit that joy, accord,
Which commeth by the Favour of the Lord.

    God's Favour ever highly estimate,
    As the prime motive of tru happinesse,
    Whereof, since that thou didst participate,
        In Life or Death, feare no kind of distresse;   [70]
When humane help shall fayl thee utterly
Then is Gods saving opportunity.

    Deadnesse of spirit that thou mayst avoyd,
    The lively means of godlynesse embrace,
    And cease not seeking though thou be delayd,
        But wait till God do manifest his grace,
For thy deliverance, prefix no day,
But paciently the Lords due leisure stay.

The fourth Meditacion.

ALas my Soule, oft have I sought thy Peace,
But still I find the contrary encrease,
Thou being of a froward disposicion,
Perceivest not thy mercyfull Physician
Doth give thee for thy health these strong purgacions
So may we call our daily molestacions,
Which how to beare, that thou mayst understand
Take heed of two extreams under Gods hand,
The one is, too light takeing thy Distresse,
The other's, hopelesse Greife or Pensivenesse;   [10]
Between these two, observe with heedfull eye
A middle course or mediocrity;
Consider for the first, if one correct
His Child, who seemeth it to disrespect,
Warding the blow or setting light therby,
How is he beat again deservedly;
So if that thou should'st seem to disregard,
The Chastisments of God, or seek to ward
The same by wayes or meanes impenitent,
How just shall God renew thy punishment: [20]
If Physick for our Bodies health be tane,
We hinder not the working of the same,
Strong Physick if it purge not, putrifies,
And more augments then heales our malladies,
And as is sayd, our manifold Temptacions,
Are nothing but thy scouring Purgacions,
Wherin a dram too much, hath not admission,
Confected by so Skilfull a Physician
Who will not have their bitternesse abated,
Till thy ill humors be evacuated;   [30]
Then loose it down for thy Humilliacion,
And hinder not its kindly Opperacion,
As thou mayst by untimely voyding it
By vain contentments, which thou mayst admit,

78

Which makes us drive repentant thoughts away,
And so put far from us the Evill day;
But that content which is by such meanes got
Is like cold water, tane in fevers hot,
Which for the present, though it seem to ease,
Yet after it encreaseth the disease;   [40]
But thou dost rather unto Grief incline,
As Crosses therfore, subject to repine,
Supposing oft, thy present troubles are
Intolerable, and thy bane declare;
Whilst thou for this, thy selfe dost maserate
Dispair unto thee doth intimate,
That none hath been afflicted like to thee,
Unparaleld thy visitacions bee;
The by-waies being thus discovered,
Endeavour in the right way to be led,   [50]
With tru Repentance, hope of pardon joine,
Deny thy selfe, and trust for help divine,
Seek first with God in Christ to be at peace,
Who onely can thy Tribulacion cease,
For he that laid the Rod (affliction) on,
The power hath to pull it off alone;
Twere but in vain for one that were in debt,
To see the Officers a discharg to get,
Till with his Creditor he doth agree
He cannot walk out of his danger free;   [60]
So vain are they, which think their course is sure,
When in the use of meanes they rest secure,
Whereas if God his blessing doth restrain
We by the creature can no help attain:
Though it hath pleased God out of his grace,
Naturall causes over things to place,
Yet keeps he to himselfe, (blest be his name)
The staffe and operacion of the same;
Then do not think my Soule to find redresse
By meanes of Freinds, or by self-Skilfulnesse,   [70]

79

But rather all created helps deny,
Save as they serve for God to work thereby:
Now forasmuch as God is just alone,
Know, without cause he hath afflicted none,
Sith without doubt, his wayes so equall be,
For som great fault he thus correcteth thee,
Therfore to lowest thoughts thy self retire,
To seek the cause that moved God to ire,
Which when thou findest, whatsoere it be
As thy right hand or eye so dear to thee,   [80]
Resolve for ever to abandon it,
Be watchfull lest the same thou recommit,
Renew thy Covenant with God, and vow
In the remainder of thy dayes, that thou
Wilt walk before him with an upright heart
If for that end his grace be on thy part,
If when hereto thou dost thy forces try,
In them thou find a disability,
Then look to Christ, who doth thy weaknesse veiw
And of compassion will thy strength renew,   [90]
From him alone thou mayst that grace derive
Which like a Cordiall or Restorative,
Will strengthen and repair thy faculties,
Which else are dead to holy exercise,
Twill make thy Understanding apprehend
God as a Father, who in Love doth send
Correction to his Children when they stray,
When without check the wicked take their sway;
This grace once tasted, so affects the will,
As it forsaketh that which cannot fill;   [100]
The well of living waters, to frequent,
Can onely fill the Soule with tru content;
The memory it doth corroberate,
To keep a store, the Soule to animate,
Gods precious promises the treasures be,
Which memory reserves to comfort thee;

The over-flowings of this grace divine
To goodnesse the affections will encline,
Turning the hasty current of thy love
From things below, unto those things above,　　　　　[110]
Seeing it is the grace of Christ alone,
Which makes the Soule to be with God at one,
Endeavour for it, give thy selfe no rest,
Till feelingly thereof thou be possest.

The fifth Meditacion.

SUch is the force of each created thing,
That it no solid happinesse can bring,
Which to our minds may give contentments sound
For like as *Noahs* Dove no succour found,
Till shee return'd to him that sent her out,
Just so the Soule in vain may seek about,
For rest or satisfaction any where,
Save in his presence, who hath sent her here.
Gods omnipresence I do not deny,
Yet to the Faithfull he doth spec'ally,　　　　　[10]
Alone his gracious presence evidence,
Who seeing all true blessings flow from thence,
Are troubled onely when he hides his Face,
Desiring still to apprehend his Grace,
This Grace of God is taken diversly
And first it doth his Favour signify,
That independent Love of his so free,
Which mov'd him to his mercyfull Decree,
His *Merum beneplacitum* it is
That's motive of all good conferd on his:　　　　　[20]
The fruits of this his Love or Favour deare,
Are likewise called Graces every where,

Election and Redempcion, graces are,
And these his Favour cheifly do declare.
Faith, Hope, Repentance, Knowledg, and the rest,
Which do the new Creac'on manifest,
Now these are counted Grace habituall.
And lastly, this the Grace of God we call,
His actuall Assistance on our side,
Wherby we overcome when we are tride;   [30]
How ever then the word is understood
Grace is the cheif desirable good.
Tis *Summum bonum*; is it so? for why?
Because without it no Prosperity,
Or earthly Honours, in the high'st degree,
Can make one truly happy sayd to be,
For as we might their miseries condole
Who should inhabit neare the Northern-Pole,
Though Moon & Stars may there apear most bright
Yet while the Sun is absent, still tis night,   [40]
And therfore barren, cold, and comfortlesse,
Vnfit for humane creatures to possesse:
More fruitlesse, empty comfort is the Mind,
Who finds the Sun of Righteousnesse declind.
Yea, though all earthly glories should unite
Their pomp and splendor, to give such delight,
Yet could they no more sound contentment bring
Then Star-light can make grasse or flowers spring;
But in that happy Soule that apprehends
His Loving kindnesse, (which the Life transcends)   [50]
There is no lack of any thing that may
Felicity or tru delight convey;
As whilst the Sun is in our Hemisphere,
We find no want of Moon nor Star-light cleare,
So where the Fountain of tru Light displayes
His beames, there is no need of borrow'd joyes,
For where he is who made all things of nought,
There by his presence still fresh joyes are wrought

Nor need he help to make a happy one,
Sith all perfection is in him alone,   [60]
Grant then his Grace is most to be desir'd
And nothing else to be so much requir'd;
But here a carnall crew are to be blam'd,
By whom the Grace of God so much is nam'd
Who are experienc'd in nothing lesse
As do their course and practises expresse,
For though they say the Grace of God's worth all
Yet will they hazzard it for Trifles small,
Hereof they'll put you out of all suspicion
When Gods Grace coms with mens in competicion   [70]
For holy duties lightly such neglects,
Whereby Gods Love is felt with its effects,
The favour of a mortall man to gain
Though but a shew thereof he do attain,
And that perhaps for some employment base
Which one cannot perform and keep tru Grace,
Therefore tis probable, how ere they prate,
Gods Grace they value at too low a rate
For to be purchast by them, sith they leave
Their hold of it, a shaddow to receave;   [80]
But they that do in truth of heart professe
That they have found this Pearle of Blessednesse
Will not adventure it for any thing,
Whatever good it promiseth to bring,
Because they know the choisest quintesence
Of earthly pleasures greatest confluence,
Cannot procure that sweet blissefull peace
Which from Gods Favour ever takes encrease;
Yet many times it comes to passe we see,
That those who have tru grace so senslesse be   [90]
Of it, that they in seasons of distresse,
Abundance of impacience do expresse,
But tis their sin, and brings an ill report
Upon their cheifest Comfort, Strength and Fort;

Such therefore should endeavour paciently,
To beare whatever crosse upon them ly,
And that by strength of this consideracion
That they have need of this theyr tribulacion   1 *Pet* 1.6.
It may be to mind them of some offence
Which they committed have (perhaps) long since   [100]
Yet they remaine unhumbled for it,
Or elce (may be) some Duty they omit,
In which remissive course they will remain,
Till with a Rod they be brought home again;
Or if they would consider how they prove
The Lords great Pacience towards them, and Love
In wayting for theyr turning to his wayes,
They would not think so greivous of delayes,
Of restitucion to that solace sound,
Which in the sence of Grace is ever found,   [110]
Which whoso will in Heart and Life preserve,
These following directions must observe;
The first is, to purge out inniquities
With all that might offend Gods puer eyes,
The next is, to have Faith in Christ, and Love
Of God, and that which he doth best approve;
Humility must likewise have a place
In them that will be sure of tru Grace,   *Iam.* 4.6
Then there must be sincear Obedience
To all *Jehovah's* just Commandements,   [120]
For God will manifest himself to those,
Who by Obedience, Love to him disclose.   *Ioh.* 14
Now lastly, that which fits one to embrace
The sence of God's exceeding Love and Grace
Is skilfulnesse in that most blessed Art
Of walking with the Lord with upright heart,
That is to manage all things heedfully,
As in the veiw of Gods omniscient eye,
And so, by consequence, by Faith to joyne
In union with the Trinity divine;   [130]

84

This is the very life of happynesse,
Which one may feel far better then expresse:
But left whilst being wrapt above my sphere,
With sweetnesse of the Theame, I should appeare
Quite to forget the nature of a Song,
And to some this might seem over-long,
My thoughts theyr workings, speedily suspends,
And at this time my Meditacion ends.

Finis.

Verses on the twelvth Chapter
of *Ecclesiastes.*

All Earthly Glories to theyr periods post,
As those that do possesse them may behold,
Who therfore should not be at too much cost
With that which fades so soon, dies & growes old
　　But rather minde him in their youthfull dayes,
　　Who can give glory which shall last alwayes.

Ere Light of Sun or Moon or Stars expire,
Before the outward sence eclipsed be,
Which doth direct the heart for to admire
These works of God which obvious are to see,　　　　[10]
　　The Fabrick of the Earth, the Heavens high,
　　Are to the mind discoverd by the eye.

Again, before the strong men, low shall bow,
And they that keep the house shall tremble sore
Ere natures force be spent, or quite out-flow;
And wonted courage shall be found no more,
　　When weaknesse shall each part emasculate
　　And make the stoutest heart effeminate.

85

Moreover, ere the grinders shall be few
Which for concoction doth the food prepare,   [20]
And Dames of musick shall be brought so low
That for their melody none much shall care;
    Harsh and unpleasant, then the voyce shall bee
    The breast being not from obstructions free.

Also before that, causlesse feares arise,
By reason of much imbecility,
Conceit of harmes will in the way surprise
Such feeble ones, which would from shadowes fly
    When chilling Frost of sad decrepid age,
    The force of vitall vigour shall aswage.   [30]

The Almond Tree shall blossoms then declare,
Gray hairs presage to them the end is nigh,
Naturall heat having no more repaire,
Desires fayle, as flames wanting fuell, dy,
    Nothing remayning wherby strength's suppli'd
    The marrow wasted, and the moysture dri'd.

And ere the silver cord be loose and weak,
Before the veins be stopt, and sinews shrink
And ere the golden Bowl or Pitcher break,
Before the heart for want of spirit shrink   [40]
    The head whereas the animals reside,
    Now full of maladies, and stupyfide.

The Body thus out-worn and quite decayd,
The dust returneth to the Earth again;
To God who gave it, is the Soul convayd
Who doth with it as he did preordain,
    How ever som to vent their falacy
    Conclude the Soul doth with the Body dy.

Which if were truth, why did our Saviour say?
Feare him not which the Body kils alone,   *Mat.* 10.28.
And hath no might the Soul for to destray,   [51]
If with the one the other must be gone;
    But that they may declare impostors skill
    Twixt Soul and Spirit they distinguish will.

The Soul (say they) doth with the Body dy,
Then there's a third part which they Spirit call,
Who doth return to God immediatly
Leaving the Dead till judgment-generall,
    And then returning breathing doth infuse
    In Soul and Body, wherby life ensues.   [60]

For which they have no Scripture (I suppose)
Save what they wrest unto theyr own Perdicion,
As this, where 'tis said, the word with power goes
Twixt Soul & Spirit by divine commission   *Heb.* 4. 12.
    Twixt joynts and marow it doth penetrate,
    Seeing all secrets, heart can meditate.

The joynts and marrow of the Body be
Not sev'rall species, but of kind the same,
The Body to support, each part agree,
And ev'ry member hath its sev'rall name;   [70]
    So Soul and Spirit is one entire thing,
    Immortall by the vertu of its Spring.

More texts of Scripture these Deceivers wrest,
Which should be answered, Truth for to defend;
But seeing here I have so long digrest,
What I begun, I hasten now to end,
    Which is to stir up youth their God to mind,
    Before effects of evill dayes they find

All here is Vanity the Preacher sayes,
Yea use of many books are wearisome,   [80]
If cheifly don for self-respect or prayse
It doubtlesse will to such a snare become:
    Of all the matter, then the End let's hear,
    Keep Gods commandements with son-like fear.

FINIS.

Notes

Textual Notes

The Discourse (8)

10 My] Me
262 imploydl] implyd
572 fruits] friuts
573 fruits] friuts
574 needs] deeds

A Song expressing their happinesse (31)

85 [Lust]: The brackets are in the original, and the initial letter is not
clearly printed. "Lust" is the best conjecture.

A Song shewing the Mercies of God to his people (35)

21 This line is partially cut off by the top of the page, but only the final
word, "passed," is conjectural. To keep with the metrical pattern, it
should be sounded as two syllables.

A Song declaring that a Christian may finde tru Love (37)

47 There seems to be a one syllable word missing from this line. conj: Yet
are their hearts most *foul* (they trow)

A Song exciting to spirituall Alacrity (47)

32 This line is not indented in the original.

Another Song exciting to spirituall Mirth (49)

3–23 The first letter or letters in each of these lines is partially or wholly
cut off by the edge of the page. Some of my conjectural restorations
rely on Brydges and Dyce.

18 Let] Norbrook and the Women Writers Project text both print: Yet. Brydges and Dyce print: Let. I agree with the latter because the tone of the poem is more conditional and monitory than confident and assured.

This Song sheweth that God is the strength (51)

71–90 The first letter in each of these lines is partially or wholly cut off by the edge of the page.

89 Thy] The "h" in this word is partly visible, which makes the Women Writers Project text's conjectural "Any" unacceptable.

Another song [The Winter] (55)

2–5 The first letter or letters in each of these lines is partially or wholly cut off by the edge of the page.

2 I then] Greer (151) and Wilcox (67) both print "When." Stewart, in *The Enclosed Garden* (106), and the Women Writers Project text print "then." The sentence requires a subject and the line requires another syllable, so I emend to "I then."

60 Greer says "The last line is missing from the copy text, 'Can e'er define' completes the sense" (154). But the last line is clearly printed in the Huntington Library copy, although it is partially cut off in the *Early English Books* microfilm series and in Stewart's facsimile.

Another Song [Time past] (63)

26–53 The first letter or letters in each of these lines is partially or wholly cut off by the edge of the page.

47 First] Part of what may be an "r" is visible at the edge of the page, making "First" more plausible than the Women Writers Project text's conjectural "Test." "First" may also be logically followed by "Then" in line 49 (also conjectural).

51 With] Part of what may be a "t" is visible at the edge of the page, making "With" more plausible than the Women Writers Project text's conjectural "Such."

The fourth Meditacion (78)

67 It is difficult to determine if the comma in this line is inserted by hand or simply printed imperfectly. I retain it.

Commentary

In referring to Collins' poems in the commentary, I use abbreviated titles except in cases where the full title is necessary to illustrate a particular point. Biblical quotations are from the King James Version, which seems to be closer to Collins' phrasing than the Geneva Bible.

Title page

Printed by R. Bishop: Richard Bishop was a London printer who, according to Plomer, operated at St. Peter's Pauls Wharf from 1631–1653, taking over William Stansby's business (p. 25). The titles that came from Bishop's shop are widely varied, including works by Ben Jonson, Richard Sibbes, Robert Farley, John Selden, Richard Brathwait, and Richard Hooker, and it is difficult to glean from his list whether his work reflected any particular political or religious affiliation or orientation.

To the Reader (1)

3 Collins describes her early years of suffering in more detail in "The Preface," lines 1–21 (see also 99–112 for a description of the transition from weakness to strength), and "The Discourse," 58–91. On physical decay allied to spiritual health as a theme in women writers, see Purkiss.

3–4 For Collins' strong defense of her poems, see "The Preface," 78–98.

6 *affected*: fondly attached, inclined to

12 For further comments on "plesant histories" see "The Discourse," 106–19.

17 The volume follows this structural plan, opening with "The Discourse," Collins' longest poem, followed by thirteen songs and five meditations. The only poem not taken specifically into account by this description is the concluding one, a verse commentary on a chapter from Ecclesiastes.

22 Hebrews 13:5: "for he hath said, I will never leave thee, nor forsake thee."

23 Romans 8:28: "And we know that all things work together for good to them that love God, to them who are the called according to his purpose."

24 *experimentally*: by experience. Throughout the volume Collins discusses the problem of assurance, noting that even a holy person is not always fully convinced of his or her salvation. See, for example, "The Discourse," 526–68.

The Preface (3)

As Greer notes (p. 150), "The Preface" is written in rime royal (7-line stanzas of iambic pentameter, rhyming ABABBCC), a form used by King James (hence its name) but also in various devotional and discursively meditative poems, such as Milton's "On the Morning of Christ's Nativity" and "The Passion," and "The Penitent Publican" by Thomas Collins (relationship to An Collins unknown).

1 *weakness*: See "To the Reader," 1–5.

3 *want of wakeing mind*: lack of alertness, lethargy

5 For a biblical warning against sleep, see 1 Thessalonians 5:6: "Therefore let us not sleep, as do others; but let us watch and be sober."

9 *intellectuals*: mental powers (Greer, p. 151) *vent*: express

15–21 The principle of accommodation, that God communicates in different ways according to the capacity of the person addressed, was commonplace. See, for example, Milton's *Paradise Lost*, Books V and VI, and *The Christian Doctrine*, Chapter 2 (pp. 905–06).

18 Collins may be echoing Romans 16:25 on the progressive "revelation of the mystery, which was kept secret since the world began."

19 Revelation 6 describes the opening of six seals, preparatory to the coming of the Lamb of God in judgment (the seventh is not opened until chapter 8), and concludes by announcing "the great day of wrath is come." There are other apocalyptic references in Collins (e.g., "Song: Civill War," 89–100).

22 *wise*: ways. Augustine stresses the contrast between Old Testament law and New Testament gospel (see Collins' line 29), and so do Luther, Calvin, and other Protestants following him.

24–28 Collins continues to echo Revelation 6, with references to terrifying catastrophes, God as an "avenger" (6:10), and the astonishing appearance of an ominous "pale horse" (6:8), carrying Death on its back. See also 1 Thessalonians 4:4–6 for the Lord as "the avenger" of lust, fornication, and other types of wickedness, and Exodus 20:5: "for I the Lord thy God am a jealous God"

94

26 *workes*: causes

27 *holden*: held

31 *good tydings*: a literal translation of the Greek word evangelist (see "Evangelicall," 34), denoting one who announces the good news about Christ. See Luke 2:10: "I bring you good tidings of great joy."

36 *plenerie*: fullness. See Galatians 4:4–6: "But when the fullness of the time was come, God sent forth his Son, made of a woman, made under the law, to redeem them that were under the law."

43 *Sonne of Righteousnesse*: Malachi 4:2: "But unto you that fear my name shall the Sun of righteousness arise with healing in his wings." The last book of the Old Testament concludes with this prefiguration of the Christ of the New Testament.

49 Isaiah 40:11: "He shall feed his flock like a shepherd: he shall gather the lambs with his arm, and carry them in his bosom, and shall gently lead those that are with young."

55 *apprehensions*: sensory reception, awareness

57–70 Topical allusions to troublesome innovators and time–servers set this poem squarely in a context of theological and political controversy.

67 *best Treasures*: See Matthew 6:19–21 on the imperishable "treasures in heaven" and the corruptible and "treasures upon earth."

68–77 Although suspicious of innovation (see 13–14, 57–70), Collins argues here and elsewhere that religion can indeed grow and develop (see, for example, "Time past we understood by story"). She further allows for the legitimacy of the religious experience of the "greater Light," perhaps an allusion to the Quakers and other sects who treated the individual's direct experience of the "inner light" as a central proof or "commendacion" of Christianity (see note on "The second Meditacion," 47). But she seems more comfortable with the time-tested, traditional experience and expression of Christianity: God appearing to the community of saints through Scripture, "Gospel-voyce." On scriptural and extrascriptural Protestantism, see Nuttall. On the Quakers, see Braithwaite and Reay.

74 *probatum est*: it has been proved (a term from logic)

78–98 Healy, pp. 49–52, compares (and contrasts) this section of Collins' "Preface" to Herbert's "Jordan" (I). For Collins' strong statement of her intent not to stay silent, see lines 92–98.

79 Poems are frequently imagined as "the ofspring of my mind," especially in volumes by women; see, for example, Rachel Speght, "The Epistle Dedicatory," *Mortalities Memorandum* (1621), A2ᵛ, and the anonymous *Eliza's Babes* (1652). For further examples, see Crawford, p. 226.

82 *they may go behind*: placed farther back in line; valued less

95

88–89 Collins notes the importance of a typological approach to spiritual history, using the past (especially as contained in biblical stories) to understand the mysteries of the present. On typology in general, see Madsen; on Protestant uses of typology, see Lewalski, pp. 111–44.

92–93 For other statements of her refusal to be silent, see "Song: vanities of Earthly things," 1–4, and "Song: Civill Warr," 17–24.

95 For further mention of divine help in writing, see lines 127–28.

106 *springing*: enlivening (see "the Spring of Light," 102)

111 *vertue*: strength, efficacy

114 *spider generacion*: a reference both to the effect of a spider's digestion and to a generation of spiders, her wrong-headed contemporaries

114–26 Allegorical use of the spider and the bee was common (e.g., Bacon, *Novum Organon*, Book I, XCV). The designation of her intended audience as "the humble sort" may also continue her witty play with the figure of a bee: in the seventeenth century bumble bees were commonly called humble bees (because of their humming sound).

117 *lighting*: alighting, setting down

127–33 The language in the concluding stanza echoes several biblical psalms expressing the speaker's awareness of living in inhospitable surroundings and the need to depend on God as a rock (e.g., Psalms 18, 28, 42, 62, 71).

The Discourse (8)

On the form of rime royal, used here, see the opening note to "The Preface."

18–21 Compare Herbert's "Obedience" — "How happie were my part, / If some kinde man would thrust his heart / Into these lines" (41–43) — and Vaughan's response in "The Match."

32 Psalm 8:2: "Out of the mouth of babes and sucklings hast thou ordained strength because of thine enemies, that thou mightest still the enemy and the avenger."

34 *profound*: learned. For further comments on the theme of proper knowledge, see the notes on lines 198 and 244–45.

40 The parable of the talents in Matthew 25:14–30 was referred to repeatedly by Protestant writers and preachers, emphasizing the need to use and spread, rather than hoard and preserve, whatever was given by God.

91 *preconceipt*: anticipation (Wilcox, p. 69)

98 *speed*: prosper, succeed, reach one's goal

99 *proceed Methodicall*: Collins may simply mean that she proposes to move ahead in an orderly manner, but "Method" was a technical term from

the art of logic having to do with the proper disposition of evidence and arguments, and the theoretical and practical aspects of this topic were of serious concern to such philosophers as Ramus, Bacon, and Descartes. Greer (pp. 150–51) suggests that Collins may be referring specifically to the "Short Method for Meditation" in François de Sales, *Introduction to the Devout Life*.

103 *pleasing exercise*: Collins describes a meditative exercise intended to calm one's fears and settle one's thoughts by using a sensory experience, in this case hearing, to prompt an examination of the spiritual meaning and value of every day. Some of the most well-known and widely practiced meditative methods were Roman Catholic, based on writings by de Sales and Ignatius Loyola (see Martz), but there were Protestant meditative techniques as well (see Lewalski).

108 *unsound*: unhealthy, but perhaps also a pun: she is describing the typical "profanenesse" she hears during the day

112 *plesant histories*: secular stories, perhaps prose or verse romances. Compare her reference to "prophane Histories" in "To the Reader," 12.

123 *morning starr*: associated with the coming of Christ; see Revelation 2:28.

126 Malachi 4:2: see note on "The Preface," 43

145 Hebrews 3:19: "So we see that they could not enter in [to his rest] because of unbelief."

160 Psalm 30:5: "For his anger endureth but a moment; in his favour is life: weeping may endure for a night, but joy cometh in the morning."

163 *recolected*: gathered, restored, perhaps also with the connotation of recalled. Like Vaughan in "The Retreate," Collins may be suggesting that the individual soul moves away from a firmament of happiness and security, and yet may recover "this blissfull peace."

180 *ceard*: sealed up, perhaps with an intimation of being scarred

182 Ecclesiastes 2:26: "For God giveth to a man that is good in his sight wisdom, and knowledge, and joy: but to the sinner he giveth travail, to gather and to heap up, that he may give to him that is good before God. This also is vanity and vexation of spirit."

194 *Orient*: bright, like the sun

198 For further comments on the importance of knowledge in devotion, see "Having restrained Discontent."

203 Romans 10:2–3: "For I bear them record that they have a zeal of God, but not according to knowledge. For they being ignorant of God's righteousness, and going about to establish their own righteousness, have not submitted themselves unto the righteousness of God."

205 Compare Donne's *Satire III*, urging the reader to "Seek true religion" (line 43).

212 Romans 1:20: "For the invisible things of him from the creation of the world are clearly seen, being understood by the things that are made, even his eternal power and Godhead; so that they are without excuse." This biblical reference does not seem directly related to Collins' lines here, but supports her general emphasis on the need to know God rightly.

214 James 1:17 glosses Collins' lines 213–14: "Every good gift and every perfect gift is from above, and cometh down from the Father of lights, with whom is no variableness, neither shadow of turning."

215 1 Corinthians 8:4: "We know that an idol is nothing in the world, and that there is none other God but one."

216 1 John 5:7: "For there are three that bear record in heaven, the Father, the Word, and the Holy Ghost: and these three are one."

231 Isaiah 53:8 glosses Collins' lines 230–31: "He was taken from prison and from judgment: and who shall declare his generation?"

233 1 John 5:7: see note to line 216.

234 1 John 1: "In the beginning was the Word, and the Word was with God, and the Word was God."

244 See Psalm 26:7: "That I may publish with the voice of thanksgiving, and tell of all thy wondrous works." Also, Job 37:14: "stand still, and consider the wondrous works of God."

244–45 Collins stresses the importance of knowledge, but like Milton's Raphael in *Paradise Lost* (VIII, 159–78) warns against vain speculation. This dual message is found in Deuteronomy 29:29: "The secret things belong unto the Lord our God: but those things which are revealed belong unto us and to our children for ever."

254 Ephesians 2:1: "And you hath he quickened, who were dead in trespasses and sins."

274 See Genesis 1:26: "And God said, Let us make man in our image, after our likeness."

281 *bleared*: dimmed

283 *ceared*: see note to line 180

286 The primary biblical reference here is probably Romans 7:23: "But I see another law in my members, warring against the law of my mind, and bringing me into captivity to the law of sin which is in my members." But the phrasing may also call to mind the well-known ancient fable of "The Belly and the Members," found in Livy and Plutarch, where an implicit comparison is made between individual disarray (specifically, the revolt of body parts) and the disruption of the traditional social and political hierarchies (see also "Time past we understood by story," 33–35, for another possible allusion to this tale). For a discussion of the

political uses of this fable, see Patterson, especially pp. 111–37.

289 For this curse see Genesis 3:14–24.

291 *eschew*: avoid, renounce. Collins may be punning here: a person fore-warned about the consequences of sin should "eschew" rather than chew this "bitter root."

309 1 John 1: see line 234 above.

312 Hebrews 2:16: "For verily he took not on him the nature of angels; but he took on him the seed of Abraham."

313 *insident*: incident, included in

331 Hebrews 7:15: verses 14–16 are relevant: "For it is evident that our Lord sprang out of Juda; of which tribe Moses spake nothing concerning priesthood. And it is yet far more evident: for that after the similitude of Melchisedec there ariseth another priest, Who is made, not after the law of a carnal commandment, but after the power of an endless life." Although Greer (p. 148) speculates that Collins may be Catholic, the emphasis here on Christ's "Full satisfaction" for man's sin and "continuall intercession" is typically Protestant, and at least implicitly counters the Catholic stress on repeated sacrifices and human intercessors. Greer rightly notes that Collins is in some respects an anti-Calvinist, but her argument that she is Catholic is not convincing.

353–54 Collins' inverted sentence structure makes these lines difficult to follow. The sense is that in the hearts of those whom he intends to glorify, our savior erects a kingdom of grace.

366 2 Thessalonians 3:2: "[pray for us] that we may be delivered from unreasonable and wicked men: for all men have not faith."

379 God hammering on the human heart is a common image in devotional poems and is often pictured in emblems. See Donne's Holy Sonnet "Batter my heart."

381 *seduced*: led away, the Latin root sense

384 Collins uses both "vertu" and "virtue," usually referring to strength or power. Here, though, she seems to refer to a moral quality.

387 See Psalm 19:7–9: "The law of the Lord is perfect . . . The Statutes of the Lord are right, rejoicing the heart: the commandement of the Lord is pure, enlightening the eyes. The fear of the Lord is clean, enduring for ever."

400 *wrot*: wrought, written

401 *two Tables*: Traditionally the commandments are thought of as divided into two sections, covering duties to God and duties to society. See McGee.

405 *Touch stone*: a stone used to test the purity of gold or silver when rubbed against it. Compare to Herbert's "The Elixir."

411 *creature*: human being

433 *carnall recreations*: traditional sports, games, and enjoyments. There was a great deal of controversy about such recreations throughout the early to mid-seventeenth century, with King James and Charles issuing proclamations titled the *Book of Sports* encouraging such activities and many puritans resisting and calling for a more strict governance of the Sabbath as a day of worship. Collins apparently leaned toward the latter. For a good overview of the conflict, see Marcus.

443 Collins may be echoing Romans 1:29, where debate is listed alongside wickedness, envy, murder, and deceit as a sign of the reprobate mind. See Hornsby.

470 *mocions*: inclinations, thoughts

471 Romans 7:7: "What shall we say then? Is the law sin? God forbid. Nay, I had not known sin, but by the law: for I had not known lust, except the law had said, Thou shalt not covet." This passage is part of a complicated argument in Romans stating that the old law is dead, but that this by no means allows for antinomianism, the free indulgence in what the law prohibited.

478 *withall*: thereby

493 *orders*: the stages one passes through from being crushed by sin to ultimate release from this burden. The following stanzas describe these stages.

500 *eke*: also

503–04: Psalm 42:1 "As the hart panteth after the water brooks, so panteth my soul after thee, O God." The hart is literally a deer, but the pun on "heart" is particularly important. This verse was frequently illustrated in emblem books. See, for example, Francis Quarles, *Emblemes* (1635), Book 5, emblem 11.

513 *most prevailing known*: Perhaps Collins is here indicating her preference for the use of common (prevalent) prayers, particularly those recommended by the various directions for worship issued by the controlling Presbyterian majority during the 1640s and 1650s. By contrast, many more radical Protestant sects of the seventeenth century rejected so-called "set" prayers, whether of the Established/Anglican or Presbyterian Church, in favor of spontaneous individual prayers.

514 *ejacculacions*: ejaculations, fervent expressions. Herbert's volume of poems *The Temple* was subtitled *Sacred Poems and Private Ejaculations*.

569 Justification was one of the stages of the *ordo salutis*, the order of salvation that was much discussed by Protestant preachers and writers; see Wallace, especially pp. 43–55. In sections that follow Collins discusses other stages as well, including Sanctification, Regeneration, and

Glorification, and elsewhere she discusses Calling, specifically her calling to poetry. Conspicuous by its absence is any extensive treatment of the first step in the traditional Calvinist *ordo salutis*, Predestination or Election.

574 *deeds*: perhaps should read "needs"

576 *gilt*: guilt, with perhaps a pun on gilt as in gold or false-gold covering or decoration

578–79 A direct statement of the fundamental Protestant emphasis on grace and faith, and a sharp critique of those, like Roman Catholics, who believe in the efficacy of "our works." She returns to this topic in 603–16.

585 The correct reference is Isaiah 1:18: "Come now, and let us reason together, saith the Lord: though your sins be as scarlet, they shall as white as snow; though they be red like crimson, they shall be as wool."

593 *tane*: taken

606 *disart*: desert, merit

608 See Revelation 7:14: "These are they which came out of great tribulation, and have washed their robes, and made them white in the blood of the Lamb."

610–16 Good works are irrelevant to salvation but still obligatory, defined by traditional Protestant theology as "fruits of faith," required by God; see, for example, the sections on Faith, Salvation, and Good Works in the *Book of Homilies*. Collins' argument may be aimed at some of the contemporary radical sects who claimed that grace freed one from this-worldly morals and social and charitable responsibilities.

612 *conversacion*: daily social behavior (see also 655)

627 *corrasive*: corrosive, dissolving agent

672 Ephesians 6:10–18 describes the "whole armour of God," and in particular the "shield of faith" used in the battle against "the wiles of the devil."

680–707 For other comments on the temporary success of the "wicked" and the temptation to despair of those who are "faithfull" but "fraile," see "Song: Civill Warr" and "Time past we understood by story."

708–14 Compare this section to her comments on the "ground of Truth" in "The Preface," 87, where she similarly acknowledges her preference for the old versus the new in religion, but at the same time remains receptive to truths declared by a "greater Light" (73, 86).

A *Song expressing their happinesse* (31)

1 scorched: Perhaps recalls the "black, but comely" woman in the Song of Solomon, whom "the sun hath looked upon" (1:5–6). For a discussion

of this part of the Song of Solomon, and of the spiritual and allegorical significance of scorching by the sun, see Stewart, *The Enclosed Garden*, pp. 68–74.

3 Compare to the theme of "fruitlessness" in "Song: Mercies of God."

9 *ingresse*: entrance

17 *certifide*: assured, confident

19 *concepcion*: Collins plays here and in the next few lines with the related ideas of thought and birth.

25 Isaiah 54:5: "For thy Maker is thine husband; the Lord of hosts is his name; and thy Redeemer the Holy One of Israel; The God of the whole earth shall he be called."

28 *beloved*: a common term of address in the Song of Solomon.

36–37 See John 14:18 (Wilcox, p. 69): "I will not leave you comfortless: I will come to you."

40 *undergo*: strengthen, support

47 Collins cites Philippians 4:14 but verse 13 seems more fitting: "I can do all things through Christ which strengtheneth me."

57 *shu'd*: sued

60 Song of Solomon 5:2: "I sleep, but my heart waketh: it is the voice of my beloved that knocketh, saying, Open to me, my sister, my love, my dove, my undefiled: for my head is filled with dew, and my locks with the drops of the night."

62 *remissive*: shy, withdrawn

63 See Song of Solomon 5:6 (Wilcox, p. 69): "I opened to my beloved; but my beloved had withdrawn himself, and was gone."

68 *strainth*: strength

77 1 Corinthians 1:30: "But of him are ye in Christ Jesus, who of God is made unto us wisdom, and righteousness, and sanctification, and redemption." Collins' "Purity" is not in the biblical text.

90 Galatians 5:24: "And they that are Christ's have crucified the flesh with affections and lusts."

91 Collins refers to the "ground of Truth" in "The Discourse," 708, and "The Preface," 87.

98 Song of Solomon 6:10: "Who is she that looketh forth as the morning, fair as the moon, clear as the sun, and terrible as an army with banners?"

104 A poetical description of the sanctification process defined more abstractly in "The Discourse," 624–30.

124 *erst*: formerly

138 John 15:15: "Henceforth I call you not servants; for the servant knoweth not what his lord doeth: but I have called you friends; for all things

that I have heard of my Father I have made known unto you."

141 1 Corinthians 3:21: "Therefore let no man glory in men. For all things are yours." Compare Herbert's "The Holdfast," which may be indebted to the same biblical verses.

A Song shewing the Mercies of God to his people (35)

1 See other images of winter in "Song: spirituall Mirth" and "The Winter of my infancy," and of fruitlessness in "Song: expressing their happinesse."

1-7 For background on the "waters of life" and the typological significance of this imagery, see Dickson.

10 *discovered*: uncovered, revealed

19 *fruits of righteousnesse*: hymns, prayers, songs of praise offered to god; an echo of Philippians 1:11

32 *stay*: delay

40 See Psalm 141:2: "Let my prayer be set forth before thee as incense; and the lifting up of my hands as the evening sacrifice."

49 *sence*: immediate perception

51-54 Compare the *carpe diem* plea in "Song: expressing their happinesse," 121-27.

A Song declaring that a Christian may finde tru Love (37)

17-18 Collins' focus on breakdowns within individual marriages and households caused by spiritual incompatibility and religious differences may be useful to consider in the context of the lively discussion in the 1640s of issues of marriage and divorce, in which Milton was an active contributor.

21 See Isaiah 11:6: "The wolf also shall dwell with the lamb."

25-29 See Genesis 3:15: "And I will put enmity between thee [serpent] and the woman, and between thy seed and her seed; it shall bruise thy head, and thou shalt bruise his heel." This much-quoted passage was frequently interpreted by Protestant commentators as a "proto-evangelium," an announcement of Christ, the "Seed" who would eventually "bruise" Satan's heel (see, for example, Milton, *Paradise Lost*, X, 179-90). But some commentators identified the "Seed" more broadly as the elect or the holy (see examples cited by Patrides, pp. 93-95). Here Collins leans toward the latter interpretation.

26 *womans*: One of only two uses of this word in the volume (see also "The Winter of my infancy," 29).

29 *consanguinity*: relationship by blood

31 *affinity*: relationship by marriage

33 Ishmael was the son of Abraham and his slave Hagar (Genesis 16). His brother was Isaac, born of Abraham and his wife Sarah (Genesis 17). Ishmael is cast out into the wilderness with Hagar after Sarah sees him "mocking" (Genesis 21:9) and Isaac is considered to be Abraham's legitimate heir.

35 Rebekah was the wife of Isaac, and her twin sons Jacob and Esau were jealous rivals (see Genesis 25–27).

47 See textual note. To replace the one word apparently missing here, perhaps the line should read: Yet are their hearts most *foul* (they trow)

47 *trow*: believe

52 *contraried*: opposed

53–56 See Genesis 3:15 (quoted in note to lines 25–26 above).

62 Cain, the son of Adam and Eve, killed his younger brother Abel (Genesis 4:8), and is thus the prototypical agent of "mischiefe."

73 The swallow often called to mind devotion, because of its careful nest-building, but its migratory habits made it a commonplace symbol of an untrustworthy friend. See Rowland, pp. 167–68.

80 *double*: dissemble

86 *closely handed*: secretive, uncharitable

92 *afect*: love

A Song demonstrating The vanities of Earthly things (41)

1 *sing*: rejoice, but also write poetry

2 *Syrens*: sirens, the mythological creatures whose songs lured sailors to their death. For other statements of her refusal to be silent, see "The Preface," 92–98, and "Song: Civill Warr," 17–24.

4 *sanguin complexion*: In early physiological psychology, when the "humor" or element of blood in a person was dominant, he or she would accordingly be lively and happy. See Babb.

12 See Ecclesiastes 1:2: "Vanity of vanities, saith the Preacher, vanity of vanities; all is vanity."

25–32 On the theme of misdirected intelligence, compare Herbert's "The Agonie" and "Vanitie" (I).

34 *exquisit*: exquisite, accomplished, knowledgeable

A Song manifesting The Saints eternall Happinesse (42)

7 *Rest*: refers to both remainder and ease, a commonplace pun ("rest" is used literally as "ease" in line 60)

12 *cumbered*: encumbered, burdened (pronounced with 3 syllables)

12 Hebrews 4:6: "Seeing therefore it remaineth that some must enter therin, and they to whom it was first preached entered not in because of unbelief." This verse does not seem directly relevant to Collins' poem, but the previous verses in Hebrews discuss the "rest" promised to believers, a theme of the first stanza of this poem.

13 *Salvacion*: pronounced with 4 syllables

14 2 Timothy 2:10: "Therefore I endure all things for the elect's sakes, that they may also obtain the salvation which is in Christ Jesus with eternal glory."

24 *comlinesse*: beauty, attractiveness. Collins is sensitive to criticism of anyone who is not physically attractive, and praises inner beauty and holiness instead. See "Song: tru Love only where tru Grace is," 92–95.

55 Collins is more confident about the perseverance of grace in "Song: Mercies of God," 48–50.

68 2 Timothy 4:8: "Henceforth there is laid up for me a crown of righteousness, which the Lord, the righteous judge, shall give me at that day: and not to me only, but unto all them also that love his appearing."

70 1 Peter 1:5: see 4–5: Christ's "abundant mercy" begets us "To an inheritance incorruptible, and undefiled, and that fadeth not away, reserved in heaven for you, Who are kept by the power of God through faith unto salvation ready to be revealed in the last time."

78 Matthew 14:43: "Then shall the righteous shine forth as the sun in the kingdom of their Father."

81 *impassible*: incapable of suffering

100 Hebrews 12: perhaps especially verse 22: "But ye are come unto mount Sion, and unto the city of the living God, the heavenly Jerusalem, and to an innumerable company of angels."

103 Revelation 21: The vision of "new Jerusalem" is described in verses 10–27.

106 Hebrews 12: perhaps especially verse 23: "[ye are come] To the general assembly and church of the firstborn, which are written in heaven, and to God the Judge of all, and to the spirits of just men made perfect."

113 2 Corinthians 4:17: "For our light affliction, which is but for a moment, worketh for us a far more exceeding and eternal weight of glory."

114 *dures*: endures

117 Romans 8:18: "For I reckon that the sufferings of this present time are

not worthy to be compared with the glory which shall be revealed in us."

120 Romans 6:23: "For the wages of sin is death; but the gift of God is eternal life through Jesus Christ our Lord."

124 1 John 3:3: "And every man that hath this hope in him purifieth himself, even as he is pure."

128 Hebrews 10:34: "For ye had compassion for me in my bonds, and took joyfully the spoiling of your goods, knowing in yourselves that ye have in heaven a better and an enduring substance."

132 Ecclesiastes 12:7: "Then shall the dust return to the earth as it was: and the spirit shall return unto God who gave it." This is a key text in the debate about mortalism (the belief that at death both the body and the soul die, and await a future resurrection). For Collins' most elaborate discussion and critique of mortalism, see "Verses on *Ecclesiastes*" and the note on lines 47–72.

A Song exciting to spirituall Alacrity (47)

5–8 See "Song: expressing their happinesse" for similar use of an allegorical shade and description of fruitless condition.

6 *planted*: fixed immovably

12 *convenient*: readily available, but also necessary

13 Colossians 1:9: "For this cause we also, since the day we heard it, do not cease to pray for you, and to desire that ye might be filled with the knowledge of his will in all wisdom and spiritual understanding"

15 One of Collins' occasional potentially confusing inversions: the sense is that Christ's presence expels Satan's rule.

16 Galatians 3:13: "Christ has redeemed us from the curse of the law."

21 Isaiah 32:2: "And a man shall be as an hiding place from the wind, and a covert from the tempest; as rivers of water in a dry place, as the shadow of a great rock in a weary land."

40 See Psalm 71:3: "for thou art my rock and my fortress."

41 *sist them sore*: afflict them grievously

42 2 Corinthians 12:9: "And he said unto me, My grace is sufficient for thee: for my strength is made perfect in weakness Most gladly therefore will I rather glory in my infirmities, that the power of Christ may rest upon me."

47 *Decay of parts*: decline in mental or physical functions

50 See Revelation 22:16: "I Jesus . . . am the root and the offspring of David, and the bright and morning star."

106

53–56 See the continuation of this theme of the fortunate fall in the next poem, "Song: spirituall Mirth," especially 33–34.

54 *dain'd*: given, ordained

55 *Tree of Life*: See Genesis 2:9.

56 *alone's*: only is. Only God's love sustains the soul.

Another Song exciting to spirituall Mirth (49)

1–13 For a model for the opening lines, see the Song of Solomon, especially 2:11–12 ("For, lo, the winter is past, the rain is over and gone; The flowers appear on the earth; the time of the singing of birds is come"). Not just incidental phrases and images but the larger rhythm of recovery in Collins' poem, from winter to spring, night to day, and sickness to health is indebted to the entire Song of Solomon.

9 *learn*: teach

16 *member*: bodily part

18 *Let*: See textual note.

51 *Mocions*: thoughts (as in "The Discourse," 470)

66 While Collins frequently praises the experience of joy, she is always careful to distinguish holy from low earthly pleasure. See, for example, "Song: vanities of Earthly things," especially 5–8.

66–78 This poem was printed by Brydges (pp. 124–26) and Dyce (pp. 61–63), who may have used Brydges as a copy-text, or otherwise been guided by his printing of the poem. Both leave out the last stanza, perhaps because of its focus on "Lascivious joy" and "sensuality." Although Collins is criticizing and rejecting joy and sensuality, her earlier editors may have felt that even mentioning them was indelicate for a woman poet.

72 *sequester*: separate. During the Civil War period, this highly charged term denoted the legal process by which estates of Royalists were taken from them by the Parliamentarians.

This Song sheweth that God is the strength of his People (51)

1 As Collins strives to bring order and understanding to her "straying thoughts," there are some signs of a tripartite meditative structure described by Martz (see especially pp. 25–70): memory, an active power of recollection and perception, presents images which otherwise might remain "in oblivion dead" (line 5); this "mentall store" (6) is then analyzed, which leads to powerful emotional effects on the soul; and the

poem ends with a colloquy, a direct address to the soul to depend on God as unfailing (86–90).

reduced: diminished, concentrated, but perhaps also with the added sense of returned. For another use of this word, see "Song: Civill Warr," 58.

10 See Matthew 13:45–46, which likens the kingdom of heaven to finding and sacrificing everything for "one pearl of great price."

11 See especially Isaiah 32:2 (referred to earlier in note on "Song: spirituall Alacrity," 21). This image of the rock, emphasizing the stability and protection afforded by God, is used frequently in the Bible (e.g., Psalms 40:2, 62:2, 6–7, Matthew 7:24–27). Collins does not emphasize the traditional association of rock with the establishment of the church (see Matthew 16:18): her stress is on the individual relationship of God and the believer, not mediated by a church.

12 *incoate*: inchoate, just begun

16–25 See Isaiah 32:2: "And a man shall be as an hiding place from the wind, and a covert from the tempest; as rivers of water in a dry place, as the shadow of a great rock in a weary land."

21 On Collins' use of parenthetical interjections, see "The Winter of my infancy," note on line 19.

25 *sweltish*: not listed in the *OED*, but clearly related to "swelter," indicating that one is becoming faint or overcome with either literal or emotional heat

33 John 3:8: "The wind bloweth where it listeth, and thou hearest the sound thereof, but canst not tell whence it cometh, and whither it goeth: so is every one that is born of the Spirit."

37 For water from a rock, see Exodus 17:1–6 and Psalm 78:15–16.

46 See Psalm 61:3: "For thou hast been a shelter for me, and a strong tower from the enemy."

52 The verse number has been cut off, but the reference seems to be to Zachariah 4:6–7: "Not by might, nor by power, but by my spirit, saith the Lord of hosts. Who art thou, O great mountain? before Ze-rub-ba-bel thou shalt become a plain."

54–55 Perhaps an allusion to Isaiah 40:4: "Every valley shall be exalted, and every mountain and hill shall be made low."

57 Deuteronomy 33:29: "Happy thou art, O Israel: who is like unto thee, O people saved by the Lord, the shield of thy help, and who is the sword of thy excellency! and thine enemies shall be found liars unto thee; and thou shalt tread upon their high places."

69 *imbecility*: weakness

73–75 Collins seems to suggest that grace is not limited to those predestined to salvation by God, but is freely given to all who desire it.

81 See Psalm 71:3: "for thou art my rock and my fortress."
84 *moveable*: impermanent, flighty
89 See textual note.

Another song ["The Winter of my infancy"] (55)

1 See Song of Solomon 2:11 (as in "Song: spirituall Mirth," 1–13).
2 *I then*: See textual note.
8 *Ver*: spring. In the Huntington Library copy, "her" is underlined in ink
   and "his" is written in the margin. We have no way of determining
   whose note this is, but it is an intriguing protest against or correction of
   Collins' feminizing of Ver.
   the flowery Queen: Flora (Greer, p. 153)
11 Greer notes (p. 153): "An Collins's contrast of the 'springtime of youth'
   and the springtime of spirit is a traditional device of the meditative poets
   (Stewart, [*The Enclosed Garden*], 106–108)." She also cites a similar
   poem by Elizabeth Major, in *Honey on the Rod* (in Greer, p. 184).
19 The use of a parenthetical interruption in a verse line (see also line 32),
   delaying the expression of a thought and also adding a conversational
   tone to the verse, is a technique used frequently, and to great effect, by
   Herbert (see, e.g., "Love unknown") and poets influenced by him
   (Vaughan, for example, as in "The Mutinie"). See "Song: God is the
   strength," 21.
26 *fast*: securely
26 Song of Solomon 4:12–13: "A garden inclosed is my sister, my spouse;
   a spring shut up, a fountain sealed. Thy plants are an orchard of pome-
   granates, with pleasant fruits." On the importance of imagery from the
   Song of Solomon for meditative poetry, see Stewart, *The Enclosed
   Garden*. Greer suggests that "The garden emblems of George Wither's *A
   Collection of Emblemes, Ancient and Moderne* . . . London, 1635 may have
   influenced Collins's imagery" (p. 154). Another emblem book, *Parthe-
   neiae Sacra* (1633), by the Jesuit Henry Hawkins, may be more pertinent
   because of its repeated focus on the enclosed garden.
29 *woman*: One of only two uses of this word in the entire volume (see also
   "Song: tru Love only where tru Grace is," 26).
38 *supplanted*: uprooted (Wilcox, p. 70), or replaced by plants that are not
   weeds, a pun consistent with the garden imagery throughout the poem
60 See textual note. It is unclear why this poem ends with "Finis." The
   only other two uses of the word are self-explanatory: at the end of "The
   fifth Meditacion," structuring the five meditations as a related group and
   also perhaps separating the final poem, "Verses on the twelvth Chapter

of *Ecclesiastes*," the only verse paraphrase in the volume, from all the preceding lyrics and meditations; and after the final poem, indicating the end of the volume.

Another Song ["Having restrained Discontent"] (57)

2 *Witt*: intelligence, but perhaps also poetic ability

18–20 Collins may be distinguishing between "vertue" as a moral quality (see also line 39) and "vertu" as strength.

19–42 Compare Collins' repeated stress on the connection between devotion and knowledge with that of Rachel Speght, whose poem "The Dreame," prefixed to *Mortalities Memorandum* (1621), contains a long section arguing that for women as well as men ignorance is an affliction and it is "a lawfull auarice, / To couet *Knowledge* daily more and more" (see especially pp. 5–9).

30 *enormities*: exceeding wickedness

47 Another allusion, as in "Song: God is the strength," 10, to the "pearl of great price" in Matthew 13:45–46.

Another Song ["Excessive worldly Greife" (59)

1–24 Based on these particularly haunting lines, one can speculate about but not know for sure if Collins had some particular physical disability. In any event, body images, especially ones suggesting vulnerability, are prominent throughout her poems. See, for example, "To the Reader" (1–2), "Song: tru Love only where tru Grace is" (especially 93–96), and "Song: Saints eternall Happinesse."

9–10 Compare to the opening of "Song: vanities of Earthly things," 1–4, noting her resolve not to let her songs be stifled.

18 *Damask Rose*: Damascus rose, a large and fragrant pink

21 *monstrous Clout*: mis-shapen, unnatural, rough, or ragged cloth, contrasted with the smoothness of "Lawn" cloth (line 23). "Monstrous" may be a pun on "menstruous," or, arguably, a misprint or printer's or editor's substitution for the latter word. Isaiah 30:22 urges the holy to "defile also the covering of thy graven images of silver, and thy molten images of gold" and "cast them away as a menstruous cloth." In the Geneva Bible, Isaiah 64:6 is glossed with mention of "menstruous clothes of a woman." Mack quotes a use of this image by the Puritan Thomas Shephard in his tract *The Sound Believer*: "When the soul sees that all its righteousness is a menstruous cloth, polluted with sin . . . it begins to cry out" (p. 19).

A Song composed in time of the Civill Warr (60)

Wilcox, following Stewart (see the introduction to his facsimile edition, p. iv, note 6), says that this poem in particular "is critical of the radical wing of the parliamentary movement" (p. 55). But while Collins undoubtedly does battle here with "false Worships" (36), "Carnall Liberty" (52), and "Disorders" (64), she also specifically criticizes those who enforce oaths and imprisonment (41–48), which afflict godly radicals just as surely as conservatives and Royalists, and generally identifies those in power as agents of the devil because of their enmity to the "Cause" (79), arguably the radical "Good Old Cause" of regenerating society, extending religious freedom, and in general paving the way for the reign of the godly. In these respects, this poem is a radical protest, not a protest against the radicals. For a commentary on the political dimensions of this poem, see Gottlieb.

1 Sibells: ancient prophetesses. When the restrictions on speaking and printing were eased during the Civil War period, many women found their voice as prophets, addressing and petitioning the King, Parliament, and local magistrates about a variety of issues and complaints. For a detailed examination of seventeenth-century female prophets, see Mack. See lines 17–24 for Collins' direct statement of her commitment to speaking up for the truth.

3 Parnassus was a mountain in Greece sacred to Apollo and the nine Muses, goddesses of song, poetry, arts, and sciences.

9 Deborah: A biblical prophetess and ruler (Judges 4:4). The Song of Deborah (Judges 5) highlights her militant and successful role as leader in the battle to overcome the captivity of the Israelites at the hands of Jabin and Sisera, and it ends with a triumphant vaunt "So let all thine enemies perish, O Lord" and the simple statement that "the land had rest forty years" (alluded to by Collins in line 10).

17–24 Occasionally Collins emphasizes quiet patience, often thought of as the woman's virtue par excellence (see, for example, "The second Meditacion," 49–66), but here she impatiently makes a powerful statement on the need to speak out immediately and unhesitatingly in "Truths defence." For other such statements, see "The Preface," 92–98, "Song: Mercies of God," 19–20, 31–40, "Song: vanities of Earthly things," 1–4, "Excessive worldly Greife," 9–10, 25–26, and "Time past we understood by story," 71–77.

19: her: Truth's, but perhaps a deeply felt personal reference as well.

21 glose: shine

24 Compare to the image of spotted cloth in "Excessive worldly Greife," 23–24. The foes of truth are, figuratively speaking, smooth and colorful,

but their attractive colors are not ingrained and will thus fade, leaving only foully stained cloth.

32 This proverbial expression perhaps means: And so they are enemies of life.

43 The Parliamentary government tried to use various oaths as a way to impose obedience, such as the Solemn League and Covenant of 1643 and the widely controversial Engagement oath of January 1650, a test of loyalty to the Parliamentary government. These oaths were resisted and resented by many, not only by Royalists or ex-Royalists but also by radical sects like the Quakers, as an affront to both political and religious liberty.

45 *lightsom*: cheerful

46 *Confiscacion*: Estates of Royalists were seized by Parliament, but these were not the only economic impositions of the time. Compulsory tithes paid to the established church, for example, were resisted and resented by Quakers and many other radicals as a particularly obnoxious form of confiscation.

48 *hazard*: risk, gamble. Perhaps Collins is suggesting that many were forced to risk their salvation by falsely swearing to an oath that went against their beliefs.

50 *Lady Verity*: Truth

51 True atheists and non-believers were apparently rare at this time. Collins' reference is more likely to those who followed no established, conventional, or traditional religion or church (e.g., antinomians, Ranters, or other radical sects, who believed that grace freed them from the bonds of legal and moral obligations).

52 *Carnall Liberty*: physical freedom, apparently identified by Collins with freedom to pursue immoral pleasures. In the early 1650s, radical sects and the court of Charles II in exile in France were often attacked by their enemies as immoral libertines.

58 *reduce*: return

59 *strait*: straightaway, immediately

62 *fell*: cruel, fierce

67 *Freinds*: As early as 1652 Quakers referred to themselves as "Friends in the Truth" or simply "Friends." See Braithwaite, pp. 73, 132.

69 *holy Seed*: a kind of remnant, from which Truth will be regenerated. See line 98 for a continuation of this image, and also "Time past we understood by story," 57–63.

73–74 *What*: that, which. The holy shall enjoy that promised time of peace and plenty.

79 The italicized *Cause* perhaps indicates something very specific, the

"Good Old Cause," a rallying cry for many radicals and reformers, but in general Collins refers to the cause of righteousness.

81–104 The poem ends on an apocalyptic note. Many people, including radicals and conservatives, felt that the severity of the times was a clear indication that the end of the world was near, signaled by "Propha-nesse" (81) and "strife" (85), a general illumination (91), the conversion of the Jews (93), and the final defeat of sin and all its effects, in this case pictured as "New Babell" (95). Important studies of apocalypticism include those by Firth, Hill, and Lamont.

91 *splendant*: bright

94 The revelation and fall of the "man of sin" is described in 2 Thessaloni-ans 2:3–9, one of the key apocalyptic texts, according to Hill. He points out that the "man of sin" was traditionally taken by Protestants to be Antichrist, but the referent for Antichrist, though normally the Pope, varied widely throughout the century (see pp. 78–145 for his discussion of 1640–60).

95–96 Babel is the site of the infamous tower, described in Genesis 11:1–9, a common image of human pride and the confusion that results from relying solely on "devices" of human ingenuity.

95 *defac't*: defaced, but also etymologically suggesting destroyed (literally unmade). See "The first Meditacion," 71, for a similar usage.

Another Song ["Time past we understood by story"] (63)

1–4 What in the past was known through history or allegorical story is now turned into present day reality, and the lesson of the wasting power of sin is experienced directly.

5–7 Common patriotic Protestant notion of England as particularly blessed by God.

15 *He*: Satan

16 *discry*: descry, observe

23 *traduce*: malign

24–25 Here Collins may be defending the cause of the Presbyterians, who between the First Civil War (1642–45) and Pride's Purge (December 1648) tried to restrain and reform many religious, moral, and political abuses and still work for peace, order, and reconciliation with the King.

26 *seperate and 'sturb*: split and disturb. Collins may also be glancing at the controversial topic of the separation of church and state, and implicitly criticizing those who reduce the power of the godly by urging such a separation.

29–32 Throughout the 1640s, criticism of King Charles, perhaps alluded to

113

here as "He whom the highest Title graces" (31), often took the form of attacks on his corrupt advisors, who mislead him with "false Reports" (29) and "slanders" (32). But finally the king became the direct target, and he was beheaded on January 30, 1649. We do not know when Collins' poem was written or what exact time period it describes, but its repeated mention of "execute" (21, 24) and vivid evocation of a disordered State in which the Head is dislocated from the Body (29–35) are, in the very least, highly charged.

33–35 As in "The Discourse" (see note on line 286), Collins may be echoing Romans 7:23 and the classical fable of "The Belly and the Members," a tale with political associations directly relevant to her description of rebellion here.

34 *at bate*: at odds, in conflict

36–42 Many popular pamphlets and books during this time, such as Thomas Edwards, *Gangraena* (1646), somewhat hysterically described the countryside as being overrun with sectarians characterized by dangerous schemes and innovations.

42 *fangles*: silly or trivial inventions

47 *First*: See textual note.

51 *With*: See textual note.

Fabericks: structures, buildings, things made by manufacture

55 *necessaries*: necessities

57–58 Compare to the enduring "holy Seed" in "Song: Civill Warr," 69, who will restore order and vindicate the truth.

61 *lenity*: leniency

62 For survival of trial by fire, see especially Daniel 3, the story of the deliverance of the faithful Shadrach, Meshach, and Abednego from the fiery furnace.

66–70 Compare these lines with Collins' reflections on time past and time present, the prospect of progressive revelation, and her receptivity to the "greater Light" of truth in "The Preface," 71–91.

75 *admiring*: In seventeenth-century usage, admiring often conveyed not only a sense of esteem but also a feeling of wonder or amazement.

76 See Romans 11:33: "O the depth of the riches both of the wisdom and knowledge of God! how unsearchable are his judgments, and his ways past finding out."

Meditacions (66)

This heading, in larger type than the individual titles of the poems, indicates that this begins a new section of the volume. But Collins does not always sharply distinguish songs and meditacions: at the end of "The fifth Meditacion," for example, she refers to that poem as a "Song" (line 135).

The first Meditacion (66)

1-6 The topic of the morning meditation announced here, our corrupt and sinful "natural estate," is pursued via the traditional tripartite structure, with each part corresponding to one of the three basic human faculties, listed by Collins as "The Understanding, Will, Affections" (25). The "dangerous and damnable" (14) sinful condition is first explored by rational arguments and vivid descriptions (13-60); the next section appeals to the will to change one's behavior, turning to repentance, tears, and the expulsion of sin (61-90); and the poem concludes with an appeal to the emotions, suggesting that a "Taste of blessednesse here" (97) will "stir thee up to purity, / Newness of life, and speedy Conversion / To Holinesse" (103-05).

2 Compare "The Preface," 1-10.

3 *to*: too.

11 *first fruits*: offerings made to God to acknowledge that everything comes from him. Among many biblical passages, see Exodus 22:29: "Thou shalt not delay to offer the first of thy ripe fruits, and of thy liquors: the firstborn of thy sons shalt thou give unto me."

18 The disobedience of Adam and Eve in eating the forbidden fruit of the tree of knowledge of good and evil (Genesis 3).

19-42 Collins similarly describes human creation and the fall in "The Discourse," 274-301.

34 *Curse*: See Genesis 3:14-24 for the bodily curses that were consequences of eating the forbidden fruit. Collins adds the "Soules Callamities" (39), which she considers far worse.

43 The period at the end of the previous line breaks a fuller unit of thought that continues into this next stanza. The sense is: The soul plagued by conscience often has within itself a world of torment, unless the conscience is dead and seared, in which case the soul runs into many errors.

53 *castaway*: common image for one who is spiritually alone, shipwrecked, as in 1 Corinthians 9:27. See "The Preamble" to "The second Meditacion" for a more elaborate description.

63 *repaire*: go

65 *contrite heart*: See Psalm 51:17: "The sacrifices of God are a broken spirit: a broken and a contrite heart, O God, thou wilt not despise" (also Psalm 34:18).

73 For other comments on repentance in Collins' poems, see "The Discourse" 659–72, "The second Meditacion" 85–90, and "The fourth Meditacion" 49–56.

81 For a fuller description of the process of sanctification, see "The Discourse," 617–52.

85–90 See "The Discourse," 85–90 for the devastating power of even one sin.

88 *Belial*: connotes wickedness or lawlessness; often used as a synonym for Satan. See 2 Corinthians 6:15: "And what concord hath Christ with Belial?"

94 *second death*: permanent death, without a resurrection; the death of the spirit. See Revelation 2:11, 20:12–14, 21:8. In *Mortalities Memorandum* (1621), Rachel Speght defines the second death as the "separation / Of soule, and bodie from the loue of God; / The sinners lot, iust Condemnation" (p. 15).

97 *say*: assay

100–02 Described at greater length in "A Song manifesting The Saints eternall Happinesse," especially lines 61–108.

106 *conscience*: awareness, consciousness

The Preamble (70)

7 *Jehovah*: a non-biblical term for God, combining letters from the Hebrew "Yahweh" and "Adonai."

The second Meditacion (70)

5 Psalm 19:1: "The heavens declare the glory of God; and the firmament sheweth his handywork."

6 Psalm 145:9: "The Lord is good to all: and his tender mercies are over all his works." *over*: greater than

16 *seasoned*: rendered palatable

25 *Esaus porcion*: Esau, son of Isaac, traded his valuable birthright as the eldest son to his younger brother Jacob for food (Genesis 25:29–34). He is a type of the reprobate sinner.

35 1 Timothy 6:6: "But godliness with contentment is great gain."

44 See John 14:16 for God's gift of a lifelong "Comforter" (identified as the Holy Ghost in 14:26) who "shall teach you all things, and bring all things to your remembrance."

47 For other references to the inner light, highly value by such groups as the Quakers, see "The Preface," 71–91, "The Discourse," 713–14, "Time past we understood by story," 66–70, and "The third Meditacion," 13–16.

57 Romans 8:28: "And we know that all things work together for good to them that love God, to them who are called according to his purpose."

59 Another potentially confusing inversion: Those who obtain his knowledge are without doubts

61 *repine*: complain

62 2 Corinthians 4:6: "For God, who commanded the light to shine out of darkness, hath shined in our hearts, to give the light of the knowledge of the glory of God in the face of Jesus Christ."

77 Proverbs 28:13: "He that covereth his sins shall not prosper: but whose confesseth and forsaketh them shall have mercy."

82 Proverbs 15: 8: "The sacrifice of the wicked is an abomination to the Lord: but the prayer of the upright is his delight."

84 Psalm 66: The particular verse is not specified in the marginal note, but verse 18 seems to fit best: "If I regard iniquity in my heart, the Lord will not hear me."

87 For Christ sitting at the right hand of God, an especially favored position, see Mark 12:36 and 14:62, Colossians 3:1, and Hebrews 12:2.

88 Romans 8:33 does not seem directly relevant here: "Who shall lay any thing to the charge of God's elect? It is God that justifieth." Romans 8:26–27 focuses more specifically on the intercession of the Spirit for man, Collins' topic here.

92 *palpable*: physical, enacted sins, as contrasted with sinful thoughts mentioned in the following lines

96 Psalm 84: Verse 11 fits best: "For the Lord is a sun and shield: the Lord will give grace and glory: no good thing will he withhold from them that walk uprightly."

97 See Psalm 119:71: "It is good for me that I have been afflicted; that I might learn thy statutes."

99 Psalm 119: see verse 176: "I have gone astray like a lost sheep."

106 *wants*: needs

131–32 On God's omniscience, see also "The fifth Meditacion," 128.

The third Meditacion (75)

1 See Psalm 27:14: "Wait on the Lord: be of good courage, and he shall strengthen thine heart: wait, I say, on the Lord."

5 See "The second Meditacion," 71.

8 *Commodity*: benefit

13–16 For other references in Collins to an inner light, see the note on "The second Meditacion," 47.

19–20 *Ashkelon* and *Gath*: cities of the Philistines, enemies of the Israelites and types for reprobate sinners. See 2 Samuel 1:20: David, lamenting the death of Saul, said "Tell it not in Gath, publish it not in the streets of As-ke-lon; lest the daughters of the Philistines rejoice, lest the daughters of the uncircumcised triumph." Contrast her claim elsewhere (e.g., "Song: Civill Warr," 17–24) that tales of affliction should be told to give continual testimony to the power of God to restore the godly to comfort and consolation.

33 *Iuball*: Jubal "was the father of all such as handle the harp and organ" (Genesis 4:12).

49 See Psalm 16:5: "The Lord is the portion of mine inheritance."

52 *Earnests*: guarantees

54 *Lot*: an object, typically a small stone, thrown on the ground to help one consult God

58 See Isaiah 61:10: "I will greatly rejoice in the Lord, my soul shall be joyful in my God; for he hath clothed me with the garments of salvation, he hath covered me with the robe of righteousness."

The fourth Meditacion (78)

Like "The first Meditacion," this poem is structured in three general parts, according to the human faculty addressed. It opens with a lengthy series of examples aimed at the understanding (1–72); the next section (73–102) is directed at the will and outlines some specific changes in behavior; and the poem ends emotionally (103–14), underscoring the importance of loving God and possessing him "feelingly" (114).

3 *froward*: forward, impatient

6 *molestacions*: troubles

9–10 On the dangers of taking grief too lightly or too heavily, see "The first Meditacion," 49–51.

18 *ward*: block, protect from

28 *Confected*: made

31 *loose it down*: drink it down

33 *untimely voyding*: prematurely expelling or discharging

45 *maserate*: macerate, gnaw at

46 *intimate*: tell

47–48 Compare to the imagined complaints of the carnal person in "The second Meditacion," 111–20.

85 *upright heart*: See Proverbs 11:20: "They that are of a froward heart are abomination to the Lord: but such as are upright in their way are his delight"; and 28:18: "Whoso walketh uprightly shall be saved but he that is perverse in his ways shall fall at once." Collins uses this image again in "The fifth Meditacion," 126.

80–81 See Matthew 18:8–9: "Wherefore if thy hand or thy foot offend thee, cut them off, and cast them from thee . . . And if thine eye offend thee, pluck it out, and cast it from thee" (also Matthew 5:29 and Mark 9:47).

96–97 See lines 14–20 on God as chastising his children. For another use of this patriarchal and familial image, see "Song: Mercies of God," also associated (as in this poem, 92) with the administration of "cordiall Comforts."

101 *well of living waters*: see Song of Solomon 4:15, and the note on "A Song shewing the Mercies of God to his people," 1–7.

The fifth Meditacion (81)

Like the first and fourth, this meditation also adopts the traditional tripartite structure. In lines 1–110, the main topic, God's grace, is introduced and analyzed; 111–30 address the will and outline some practical directions for living a life of grace; and the final section (131–38) turns to the emotions and concludes the poem by briefly describing the inexpressible "sweetnesse" (134) of grace that "one may feel far better then expresse" (132).

4 Noahs *Dove*: While on his ark, Noah sends out a dove to see if the flood waters had receded, "But the dove found no rest for the sole of her foot, and she returned unto him into the ark, for the waters were on the face of the whole earth" (Genesis 8:9).

19 *Merum beneplacitum*: that which is completely good and pleasing

26 The "New Creation," a commonplace in Protestant theology, is ultimately Pauline at its source. See, for example, 2 Corinthians 5:17: "Therefore if any man be in Christ, he is a new creature: old things are passed away; behold, all things are become new"; and Ephesians 4:24: "put on the new man, which after God is created in righteousness and true holiness."

33 *Summum bonum*: As Collins goes on to explain, the "cheif desirable good" (32).

44 *Sun of Righteousnesse*: Malachi 4:2; see note on "The Preface," 43.

63–80 Compare to her description of the "carnallist" in "The Discourse," 260–66 and "The second Meditacion," 19–34. Collins may have in mind religious hypocrites or perhaps radical sects like the Ranters that believed grace set one free from holy duties and laws.

82 See Matthew 13:45–46: "The kingdom of heaven is like unto a merchant man, seeking goodly pearls; Who, when he had found one pearl of great price, went and sold all that he had, and bought it."

98 1 Peter 1:6: "Wherein ye greatly rejoice, though now for a season, if need be, ye are in heaviness through manifold temptations.

99 *mind*: call attention to, remind

103 *remissive*: neglectful

114 *puer*: pure

118 James 4:6: "Wherefore he saith, God resisteth the proud, but giveth grace unto the humble."

122 John 14: The particular verse is not specified in the marginal note, but verse 21 seems to fit best: "He that hath my commandments, and keepeth them, he it is that loveth me: and he that loveth me shall be loved of my Father, and I will love him, and will manifest myself to him."

126 *upright heart*: see note on "The fourth Meditacion," 85.

133 *wrapt*: rapt, enraptured

Verses on the twelvth Chapter of *Ecclesiastes* (85)

1 *periods*: end

3 *at too much cost*: deeply involved

19 *grinders*: teeth

20 *concoction*: digestion

27 *Conceit*: imagination

31 See Ecclesiastes 12:5: "Also when they shall be afraid of that which is high, and fears shall be in the way, and the almond tree shall flourish, and the grasshopper shall be a burden, and desire shall fail." Ferguson notes that "The almond is a symbol of divine approval or favor" (p. 27), and cites Numbers 17:1–8, describing Aaron's Rod, which buds and brings forth almonds, confirming him as a priest of the Lord.

35 *strength's suppli'd*: There is a space for an apostrophe in the first word, but the apostrophe itself is missing, most likely because of bad inking. The line is no doubt meant to read: strength is supplied

41–42 *animals*: animal spirits

47–72 The original biblical text gives a powerful picture of physical decay (as does Collins), but there is no mention of the issue of whether or not the soul dies or decays as well. For Collins, this notion is a "falacy" (47). Hirst explains why mortalism was considered by some to be a dangerous heresy: "Milton, Overton, Walwyn, Winstanley and many less famous names held that the soul perished with the body, to be revived at the approaching Armageddon. Mortalism, 'soul-sleeping,' challenged the claims of all established churches to be *the* visible church, since if the saints died, the church could only be the congregations of which they were members for their time on earth. Mortalism also seemed to guarantee the end of all order, as its conservative opponents readily misidentified it with materialist atheism, and assumed that mortalists denied the existence of an after-life" (p. 289). For further discussions of mortalism, see Burns and Hunter.

50 Matthew 10:28: "And fear not them which kill the body, but are not able to kill the soul: but rather fear him which is able to destroy both soul and body in hell."

58 *judgment-generall*: the day of judgment

64 Hebrews 4:12 "For the word of God is quick, and powerful, and sharper than any twoedged sword, piercing even to the dividing asunder of soul and spirit, and of the joints and marrow, and is a discerner of the thoughts and intents of the heart." Collins sees this as a biblical source wrested from its true meaning by mortalists.

72 *Spring*: origin

79 Collins returns here to the biblical text. See Ecclesiastes 12:8: "Vanity of vanities, saith the preacher; all is vanity."

80–82 See Ecclesiastes 12:12: "And further, by these, my son, be admonished: of making many books there is no end; and much study is a weariness of the flesh." Collins thus ends this poem and her entire volume on a self-critical note. She does not renounce the usefulness of her whole project of writing, but directly acknowledges that writing may be a "snare" (82).

84 Ecclesiastes 12:13: "Fear God, and keep his commandements: for this is the whole duty of man."

Works Cited

Babb, Lawrence. *The Elizabethan Malady*. East Lansing: Michigan State College Press, 1951.

Bell, Maureen, George Parfitt, and Simon Shepherd. *A Biographical Dictionary of English Women Writers 1580–1720*. Boston: G. K. Hall, 1990.

Bibliotheca Anglo-Poetica. London: Thomas Davison, 1815.

Braithwaite, William C. *The Beginnings of Quakerism*. London: Macmillan, 1923.

Brydges, Egerton, ed. *Restituta*. Vol. 3. London: T. Bensley, 1815.

Crawford, Patricia. "Women's Published Writings 1600–1700." In *Women in English Society 1500–1800*, ed. by Mary Prior, 211–82. London: Methuen, 1985.

Dickson, Donald R. *The Fountain of Living Waters: The Typology of the Waters of Life in Herbert, Vaughan, and Traherne*. Columbia: Univ. of Missouri Press, 1987.

Dyce, Alexander. *Specimens of British Poetesses*. London: T. Rodd, 1827.

Ezell, Margaret J. M. *Writing Women's Literary History*. Baltimore: Johns Hopkins Univ. Press, 1993.

Eliza's Babes: or The Virgins-Offering. London: Printed by M. S. for Laurence Blaiklock, 1652.

Ferguson, George. *Signs and Symbols in Christian Art*. New York: Oxford Univ. Press, 1973.

Firth, Katharine R. *The Apocalyptic Tradition in Reformation Britain 1530–1645*. London: Oxford Univ. Press, 1979.

Fish, Stanley E. *Self-Consuming Artifacts: The Experience of Seventeenth-Century Literature*. Berkeley: Univ. of California Press, 1972.

Gottlieb, Sidney. "An Collins and the Experience of Defeat." In *Representing Women in Renaissance England,* ed. by Claude J. Summers and Ted-Larry Pebworth. Columbia: Univ. of Missouri Press, forthcoming.

Graham, Elspeth, Hilary Hinds, Elaine Hobby, and Helen Wilcox, eds. *Her Own Life: Autobiographical Writings by Seventeenth-Century Englishwomen.* New York: Routledge, 1989.

Greer, Germaine, and Susan Hastings, Jeslyn Medoff, and Melinda Sansone, eds. *Kissing the Rod: An Anthology of Seventeenth-Century Women's Verse.* New York: Farrar Straus Giroux, 1989.

Grundy, Isobel, and Susan Wiseman, eds. *Women, Writing, History 1640-1740.* Athens: Univ. of Georgia Press, 1992.

Hazlitt, W. Carew. *Handbook to the Popular Poetical and Dramatic Literature of Great Britain.* 1867; repr. New York, Burt Franklin, 1961.

———. *Second Series of Bibliographical Collections and Notes on Early English Literature 1474-1700.* 1862; repr. NY: Burt Franklin, 1961.

Healy, Thomas. *New Latitudes: Theory and English Renaissance Literature.* London: Edward Arnold, 1992.

Hill, Christopher. *Antichrist in Seventeenth-Century England.* Revised edition. London: Verso, 1990.

Hirst, Derek. *Authority and Conflict: England, 1603-1658.* Cambridge: Harvard Univ. Press, 1986.

Hobbes, Thomas. *Behemoth or The Long Parliament.* Ed. by Ferdinand Tönnies. Chicago: Univ. of Chicago Press, 1990.

Hobby, Elaine. *Virtue of Necessity: English Women's Writing 1649-88.* Ann Arbor: Univ. of Michigan Press, 1989.

———. "'Discourse So Unsavoury': Women's Published Writings of the 1650s." In Grundy and Wiseman, 16-32.

Hornsby, S. G., Jr. " 'Ambiguous Words': Debate in *Paradise Lost,*" *Milton Quarterly* 14.2 (1980): 60-62.

Hunter, William B. "Mortalism." In *A Milton Encyclopedia,* Vol. 5. Gen. ed. William B. Hunter, 155-56. Lewisburg: Bucknell Univ. Press, 1979.

King, Eleanor Anthony. *Bible Plants for American Gardens.* New York: Macmillan, 1941.

Lamont, William M. *Godly Rule: Politics and Religion, 1603–60.* London: Macmillan, 1969.

Lewalski, Barbara Kiefer. *Protestant Poetics and the Seventeenth-Century Religious Lyric.* Princeton: Princeton Univ. Press, 1979.

Mack, Phyllis. *Visionary Women: Ecstatic Prophecy in Seventeenth-Century England.* Berkeley: Univ. of California Press, 1992.

Madsen, William G. *From Shadowy Types to Truth: Studies in Milton's Symbolism.* New Haven: Yale Univ. Press, 1968.

Marcus, Leah S. *The Politics of Mirth: Jonson, Herrick, Milton, Marvell, and the Defense of Old Holiday Pastimes.* Chicago: Univ. of Chicago Press, 1986.

Martz, Louis L. *The Poetry of Meditation: A Study in English Religious Literature of the Seventeenth Century.* Rev. ed. New Haven: Yale Univ. Press, 1962.

Marvell, Andrew. *The Rehearsal Transprosed.* In *Andrew Marvell.* Ed. by Frank Kermode and Keith Walker, 157–273. New York: Oxford Univ. Press, 1990.

McGee, J. Sears. *The Godly Man in Stuart England: Anglicans, Puritans, and the Two Tables, 1620–1670.* New Haven: Yale Univ. Press, 1976.

Milton, John. *Complete Poems and Major Prose.* Ed. by Merritt Y. Hughes. Indianapolis: Odyssey Press, 1957.

Norbrook, David. *The Penguin Book of Renaissance Verse 1509–1659.* Ed. by H. R. Woudhuysen. New York: Penguin, 1992.

Nuttall, Geoffrey F. *The Holy Spirit in Puritan Faith and Experience.* 1946; repr. Chicago: Univ. of Chicago Press, 1992.

Patrides, C. A. *Premises and Motifs in Renaissance Thought and Literature.* Princeton: Princeton Univ. Press, 1982.

Patterson, Annabel. *Fables of Power: Aesopian Writing and Political History.* Durham: Duke Univ. Press, 1991.

Plomer, Henry R. *A Dictionary of the Booksellers and Printers ... at work in England, Scotland and Ireland from 1641 to 1667.* London: Printed for the Bibliographical Society, by Blades, East & Blades, 1907.

Purkiss, Diane. "Producing the Voice, Consuming the Body: Women Prophets of the Seventeenth Century." In Grundy and Wiseman, 139–58.

Reay, Barry. *The Quakers and the English Revolution*. New York: St. Martin's Press, 1985.

Rowland, Beryl. *Birds with Human Souls*. Knoxville: Univ. of Tennessee Press, 1978.

Speght, Rachel. *Mortalities Memorandum*. London, 1621.

Stewart, Stanley N., ed. *An Collins, Divine Songs and Meditacions* (1653). Augustan Reprint Society, number 94. Los Angeles: William Andrews Clark Memorial Library, 1961.

———. *The Enclosed Garden*. Madison: Univ. of Wisconsin Press, 1966.

Stone, Lawrence. *The Family, Sex and Marriage in England 1500–1800*. New York: Harper and Row, 1977.

Vendler, Helen. *The Poetry of George Herbert*. Cambridge: Harvard Univ. Press, 1975.

Wallace, Dewey D., Jr. *Puritans and Predestination: Grace in English Protestant Theology 1525–1695*. Chapel Hill: Univ. of North Carolina Press, 1982.

Wilcox, Helen, ed., "An Collins." In Graham, et al., 54–70. [Includes selections from Collins' poems and an introduction and notes by Wilcox.]

Renaissance English Text Society

Officers

President, Arthur F. Kinney, University of Massachusetts at Amherst
Vice-President, A. R. Braunmuller, Univ. of California, Los Angeles
Secretary, Carolyn Kent, New York, New York
Treasurer, Mario A. Di Cesare, State University of New York, Binghamton
Past President, W. Speed Hill, Lehman College, City University of New York

Council

Thomas Faulkner, University of Washington
David Freeman, Memorial University, Newfoundland
Suzanne Gossett, Loyola University of Chicago
Elizabeth Hageman, University of New Hampshire
David Scott Kastan, Columbia University
Dennis Kay, University of North Carolina, Charlotte
John King, Ohio State University
Arthur F. Marotti, Wayne State University
Steven May, Georgetown College
Janel Mueller, University of Chicago
Stephen Orgel, Stanford University
Sr. Anne O'Donnell, Catholic University of America
G. W. Pigman III, California Institute of Technology
Josephine Roberts, Louisiana State University
George Walton Williams, Duke University

International Advisory Council

Dominic Baker-Smith, University of Amsterdam
K. J. Höltgen, University of Erlangen-Nürenberg
M. T. Jones-Davies, University of Paris-Sorbonne
David Norbrook, Magdalen College, Oxford
Sergio Rossi, University of Milan
Germaine Warkentin, Victoria University, the University of Toronto

Editorial Committee for *An Collins, Divine Songs and Meditacions*:
　　John N. King, Chair
　　W. Speed Hill
　　Janel Mueller

The Renaissance English Text Society was established to publish literary texts, chiefly nondramatic, of the period 1475–1660. Dues are $25.00 per annum or $15.00 for graduate students; life membership is also available for a one-time payment of $500.00. Members receive the text published for each year of membership and may purchase other volumes at special prices. Members also receive (gratis) the volumes of collected papers from the annual meetings.

　　The Society sponsors panels at such annual meetings as those of the Modern Language Association, the Renaissance Society of America, and the conference at Kalamazoo. Membership inquiries should be addressed to the treasurer or to the appropriate member of the International Advisory Council. Other inquiries should be addressed to the president.

Publications of the Society

FIRST SERIES

VOL. I. *Merie Tales of the Mad Men of Gotam* by A. B., edited by Stanley J. Kahrl, and *The History of Tom Thumbe*, by R. I., edited by Curt F. Buhler, 1965. (o.p.)

VOL. II. Thomas Watson's Latin *Amyntas,* edited by Walter F. Staton, Jr., and Abraham Fraunce's translation *The Lamentations of Amyntas,* edited by Franklin M. Dickey, 1967.

SECOND SERIES

VOL. III. *The dyaloge called Funus,* A Translation of Erasmus's Colloquy (1534), and A *very pleasaunt & fruitful Diologe called The Epicure,* Gerrard's Translation of Erasmus's Colloquy (1545), edited by Robert R. Allen, 1969.

VOL. IV. *Leicester's Ghost* by Thomas Rogers, edited by Franklin B. Williams, Jr., 1972.

THIRD SERIES

VOLS. V–VI. A *Collection of Emblemes, Ancient and Moderne,* by George Wither, with an introduction by Rosemary Freeman and bibliographical notes by Charles S. Hensley, 1975. (o.p.)

FOURTH SERIES

VOLS. VII–VIII. *Tom a' Lincolne* by R. I., edited by Richard S. M. Hirsch, 1978.

FIFTH SERIES

VOL. IX. *Metrical Visions* by George Cavendish, edited by A. S. G. Edwards, 1980.

SIXTH SERIES

VOL. X. *Two Early Renaissance Bird Poems,* edited by Malcolm Andrew, 1984.

VOL. XI. *Argalus and Parthenia* by Francis Quarles, edited by David Freeman, 1986.

VOL. XII. Cicero's *De Officiis,* trans. Nicholas Grimald, edited by Gerald O'Gorman, 1987.

VOL. XIII. *The Silkewormes and their Flies* by Thomas Moffet (1599), edited with introduction and commentary by Victor Houliston, 1988.

SEVENTH SERIES

VOL. XIV. John Bale, *The Vocacyon of Johan Bale*, edited by Peter Happé and John N. King, 1989.

VOL. XV. *The Nondramatic Works of John Ford*, edited by L. E. Stock, Gilles D. Monsarrat, Judith M. Kennedy, and Dennis Danielson, with the assistance of Marta Straznicky, 1990.

Special Publication. *New Ways of Looking at Old Texts: Papers of the Renaissance English Text Society, 1985–1991*, edited by W. Speed Hill, 1993. (Sent *gratis* to all 1991 members.)

VOL. XVI. *George Herbert, The Temple: A Diplomatic Edition of the Bodleian Manuscript (Tanner 307)*, edited with introduction and notes by Mario A. Di Cesare, 1991.

VOL. XVII. *The First Part of the Countess of Montgomery's Urania by Lady Mary Wroth*. Ed. Josephine Roberts. 1992.

VOL. XVIII. *Solon His Follie by Richard Beacon*, ed. by Clare Carroll and Vincent Carey. 216 pp. 1993.

VOL. XIX. *An Collins, Divine Songs and Meditacions*, ed. by Sidney Gottlieb. 160 pp. 1994.

Copies of volumes X–XII may be purchased from Associated University Presses, 440 Forsgate Drive, Cranbury, NJ 08512. Copies of earlier volumes still in print or of all volumes from XIII on may be ordered from the treasurer.

The only extant copy of An Collins' poems (1653) is edited in full for the first time in this edition. Her poems are particularly interesting for their devotional framework and experimental metrical and meditative style, her allusive but bold commentary on topical events, and her challenges to the pressures imposed on a woman writer. She touches on the social and political turmoil of mid-17th-century England as well as the state of the individual soul, often incorporating personal details that add a peculiar power and engaging concreteness to her best lyrics.

Gottlieb's introduction describes the 1653 volume, its history, the editorial principles of the edition, and the contexts for understanding Collins' life and work. The commentary focuses on identifying the biblical verses Collins employs, glossing unusual words or references, and suggesting the sources of devotional/theological and topical/political matters. This volume is valuable for scholars of devotional poetry, spiritual autobiography, and women's writings of the early modern period.

Sidney Gottlieb is Professor of English at Sacred Heart University. He has published widely on An Collins and George Herbert, and is the editor of the *George Herbert Journal*. He received a fellowship from the Folger Shakespeare Library for research on this volume.

CRTS

MEDIEVAL & RENAISSANCE TEXTS & STUDIES
is the publishing program of the
Arizona Center for Medieval and Renaissance Studies
at Arizona State University, Tempe, Arizona.

CRTS emphasizes books that are needed —
texts, translations, and major research tools.

CRTS aims to publish the highest quality scholarship
in attractive and durable format at modest cost.